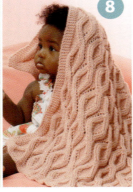

1. ⊗ Just Dandy Set 4
2. ⁄ Color Wheels Blanket 12
3. ⁄ Swirly Skirt 16
4. ⊗ Sitting Pretty Set 24
5. ⁄ Playtime Set 33
6. ⁄ Super Stripes Set 43
7. ⊗ Top Down Cuties 49
8. ⊗ Just Peachy Blankie 54

Helpful Hints 58
Skill Levels 59
Knitting Needle and Crochet Hook
Conversion Charts 59
Learn to Knit Instructions 60
Learn to Crochet Instructions 62

Like us   Follow us   Pin us   Sign up for newsletters
www.bernat.com

www.bernat.com
Every effort has been taken to ensure the accuracy of these instructions.
Bernat®, however, cannot accept responsibility for typographical errors or misinterpretation of instructions.

1. Just Dandy Set

HAT: DOUBLE-POINTED NEEDLES | LIGHT 3 | INTERMEDIATE

SIZES

Vest

To fit chest measurement	
6 mos	17" [43 cm]
12 mos	18" [45.5 cm]
18 mos	19" [48 cm]
24 mos	20" [51 cm]

Finished chest	
6 mos	19" [48 cm]
12 mos	21" [53.5 cm]
18 mos	22" [56 cm]
24 mos	24" [61 cm]

Hat

To fit baby's head: **6/12** (**18/24**) mos.

MATERIALS

Bernat® Softee® Baby™ (140 g /5 oz; 331 m/362 yds)						
Vest	**Sizes**	6	12	18	24	mos
	30044 (Flannel)	1	1	1	1	ball

Sizes 3.5 mm (U.S. 4) and 4 mm (U.S. 6) knitting needles **or size needed to obtain gauge.** Cable needle. Stitch holder. 2 buttons.

Hat	**Sizes**	6/12	18/24	mos
	30044 (Flannel)	1	1	ball

Set of four sizes 3.5 mm (U.S. 4) and 4 mm (U.S. 6) double-pointed knitting needles **or size needed to obtain gauge.** Cable needle.

ABBREVIATIONS

See page 58 for Helpful Hints.

2tog = K2tog or P2tog as appropriate
Alt = Alternate(ing)
Approx = Approximately
Beg = Beginning
C4B = Slip next 2 stitches onto cable needle and leave at back of work. K2, then K2 from cable needle
Cont = Continue(ity)
Dec = Decrease(ing)
Inc = Increase 1 stitch by knitting into front and back of next stitch
K = Knit
K1tbl = Knit next stitch through back of loop
K2tog = Knit next 2 stitches together
M1 = Make 1 stitch by picking up horizontal loop lying before next stitch and knitting into back of loop

P = Purl
P2(3)tog = Purl next 2 (3) stitches together
P2togtbl = Purl next 2 stitches through back loops
P1tbl = Purl next stitch through back of loop
Pat = Pattern
Rem = Remaining
Rep = Repeat
Rnd(s) = Round(s)
RS = Right side
St(s) = Stitch(es)
Ssk = Slip next 2 stitches knitwise one at a time. Pass them back onto left-hand needle, then knit through back loops together
WS = Wrong side

GAUGE

22 sts and 30 rows = 4" [10 cm] in stocking st with larger needles.

INSTRUCTIONS

VEST

The instructions are written for smallest size. If changes are necessary for larger sizes the instructions will be written thus ( ). Numbers for each size are shown in the same color throughout the pattern. When only one number is given in black, it applies to all sizes.

Cable Panel (worked over 12 sts). (See Chart I on page 11).
1st row: (RS). P2. (K1tbl) twice. K4. (K1tbl) twice. P2.
2nd and alt rows: K2. (P1tbl) twice. P4. (P1tbl) twice. K2.
3rd row: P2. (K1tbl) twice. C4B. (K1tbl) twice. P2.
5th row: As 1st row.
6th row: As 2nd row.
7th to 12th rows: Rep 1st to 6th rows once more.
13th row: P2. Slip next 4 sts onto cable needle and leave at back of work. K2, then knit first 2 sts from cable needle. Bring cable needle with rem 2 sts to front of work. K2, then K2 from cable needle. P2.
14th row: As 2nd row.
These 14 rows form Cable Panel Pat.

FRONT

With smaller needles, cast on **55 (**57**-**61**-**65**) sts.
1st row: (RS). *K1. P1. Rep from * to last st. K1.
2nd row: *P1. K1. Rep from * to last st. P1.
Rep last 2 rows of (K1. P1) ribbing for **1½** (**1½**-**2**-**2**) " [**4** (**4**-**5**-**5**) cm], ending with a WS row and inc **5** (**7**-**5**-**7**) sts evenly across last row. **60** (**64**-**66**-**72**) sts.

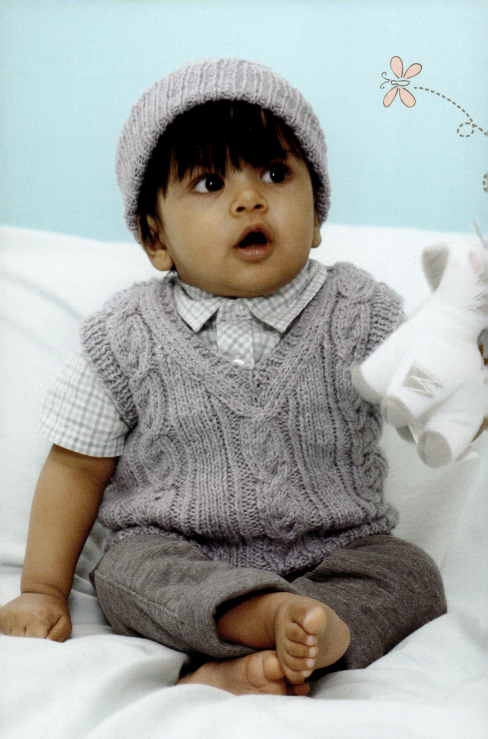

Change to larger needles and proceed in pat as follows:

1st row: (RS). K**2** (**3**-**3**-**5**). *P1. K1tbl. Work 1st row Cable Panel Pat across next 12 sts. K1tbl. P1.** K**4** (**5**-**6**-**7**). Rep from * once more, then from * to ** once. K**2** (**3**-**3**-**5**).
2nd row: P**2** (**3**-**3**-**5**). *K1. P1tbl. Work 2nd row Cable Panel Pat across next 12 sts. P1tbl. K1.** P**4** (**5**-**6**-**7**). Rep from * once more, then from * to ** once. P**2** (**3**-**3**-**5**). These 2 rows form pat. Cable Panel Pat is now in position.**

Cont in pat until work from beg measures approx **6** (**7**-**7½**-**8½**)" [**15** (**18**-**19**-**21.5**) cm], ending with a **8th** (**14th**-**14th**-**8th**) row of Cable Panel Pat.

Sizes 6 and 24 mos only: Shape armholes: Keeping cont of pat, cast off **3** (**6**) sts beg next 2 rows. **54** (**60**) sts rem.
Dec 1 st each end of next and following alt row. **50** (**56**) sts.
Work 1 row even in pat, ending on a 14th row of Cable Panel Pat.

Shape V-neck: 1st row: (RS). Pat across **19** (**22**) sts. P2tog. (K1tbl) twice. K2 (neck edge). **Turn.** Leave rem sts on a spare needle.
2nd row: P2. (P1tbl) twice. K1. Pat to end of row.

Sizes 12 and 18 mos only: Shape armhole and V-neck: 1st row: (RS). Cast off 4 sts. Pat across next (**22**-**23**) sts (including st on needle after cast off). P2tog. (K1tbl) twice. K2 (neck edge). **Turn.** Leave rem sts on a spare needle.
2nd row: P2. (P1tbl) twice. K1. Pat to end of row.
3rd row: Work 2tog. Pat to last 6 sts. P2tog. (K1tbl) twice. K2.
4th row: As 2nd row.
5th and 6th rows: Rep 3rd and 4th rows once more. (**23**-**24**) sts.

All sizes: Next row: (RS). Pat to last 6 sts. P2tog. (K1tbl) twice. K2.
Next row: P2. (P1tbl) twice. K1. Pat to end of row.
Rep last 2 rows **10** (**5**-**6**-**11**) times more. **13** (**17**-**17**-**15**) sts rem.

Sizes 12, 18 and 24 mos only: 1st row: (RS). Pat to last 5 sts. P1. (K1tbl) twice. K2.
2nd row: P2. (P1tbl) twice. K1. Pat to end of row.
3rd row: Pat to last 6 sts. P2tog. (K1tbl) twice. K2.
4th row: As 2nd row.
Rep last 4 rows (**3**-**2**-**0**) times more. (**13**-**14**-**14**) sts rem.

All sizes: Work **0** (**2**-**2**-**2**) rows even in pat.

Shape shoulder: Cast off **6** (**6**-**7**-**7**) sts beg next row. Work 1 row even in pat. Cast off rem 7 sts.

Just Dandy Set

Sizes 6 and 24 mos only: With RS facing, rejoin yarn to rem sts. K2. (K1tbl) twice. P2togtbl. Pat to end of row.
Next row: Pat to last 5 sts. K1. (P1tbl) twice. P2.

Sizes 12 and 18 mos only: With RS facing, rejoin yarn to rem sts. K2. (K1tbl) twice. P2togtbl. Pat to end of row.
1st row: Cast off 4 sts. Pat to last 5 sts. K1. (P1tbl) twice. P2.
2nd row: K2. (K1tbl) twice. P2togtbl. Pat to last 2 sts. Work 2tog.
3rd row: Pat to last 5 sts. K1. (P1tbl) twice. P2.
4th and 5th rows: Rep 2nd and 3rd rows once more. (23-24) sts.

All sizes: Next row: (RS). K2. (K1tbl) twice. P2togtbl. Pat to end of row.
Next row: Pat to last 5 sts. K1. (P1tbl) twice. P2.
Rep last 2 rows 10 (5-6-11) times more. 13 (17-17-15) sts rem.

Sizes 12, 18 and 24 mos only: 1st row: (RS). K2. (K1tbl) twice. P1. Pat to end of row.
2nd row: Pat to last 5 sts. K1. (P1tbl) twice. P2.
3rd row: K2. (K1tbl) twice. P2togtbl. Pat to end of row.
4th row: As 2nd row.
Rep last 4 rows (3-2-0) times more. (13-14-14) sts rem.

All sizes: Work 1 (3-3-3) row(s) even in pat.

Shape shoulder: Cast off 6 (6-7-7) sts beg next row. Work 1 row even in pat. Cast off rem 7 sts.

BACK
Work from ** to ** as given for Front.
Cont in pat until work from beg measures same length as Front to beg of armhole shaping, ending with the same pat row.

Shape armholes: Keeping cont of pat, cast off 3 (4-4-6) sts beg next 2 rows.
Dec 1 st each end of next row and following alt row. 50 (52-54-56) sts rem.
Cont even in pat until armhole measures same length as Front, ending with a WS row.

Shape shoulders: Keeping cont of pat, cast off 6 (6-7-7) sts beg next 2 rows, then cast off 7 sts beg following 2 rows. Leave rem 24 (26-26-28) sts on a st holder.

FINISHING
Pin pieces to measurements. Cover with a damp cloth leaving cloth to dry. Sew right shoulder seam.

V-neckband: With RS facing and smaller needles, pick up and knit 23 (30-34-30) sts evenly down left front neck edge. M1 at center of V-neck and place marker on this st for center st. Pick up and knit 23 (30-34-30) sts evenly up right front neck edge. K24 (26-26-28) from Back st holder, dec 2 sts evenly across. 69 (85-93-87) sts.

1st row: (WS). *P1. K1. Rep from * until 3 sts before marked center st. P1. K2tog. P1 (marked center st). K2tog. **P1. K1. Rep from ** to last st. P1.

2nd row: *K1. P1. Rep from * until 3 sts before marked st. K1. P2tog. K1 (marked center st). P2tog. **K1. P1. Rep from ** to last st. K1.

3rd row: *P1. K1. Rep from * until 3 sts before marked st. P1. K2tog. P1 (marked center st). K2tog. **P1. K1. Rep from ** to last st. P1.

Cast off in ribbing, dec at center as before. Place markers on left shoulder seam edges of Front and Back 1½" [4 cm] from cast off edge of V-neckband. Sew left shoulder seam to markers.

Buttonhole edging: With RS facing, pick up and knit 9 sts along unsewn edge of Front shoulder edge from marker to cast off edge of neckband.

Next row: (K2. Cast off 2 sts) twice. K1 (st left on needle after cast off).

Next row: Knit, casting on 2 sts over cast off sts.

Cast off knitwise (WS).

Armbands: With RS facing, pick up and knit 59 (63-71-79) sts evenly along armhole edge.

Beg on a 2nd row, work 5 rows in (K1. P1) ribbing as given for Front. Cast off in ribbing.

Sew side and armband seams. Sew buttons on Back left shoulder edge to correspond to buttonholes.

HAT

The instructions are written for smaller size. If changes are necessary for larger size the instructions will be written thus ( ). Numbers for each size are shown in the same color throughout the pattern. When only one number is given in black, it applies to both sizes.

Cable Panel (worked over 12 sts in rnds).

1st and 2nd rows: (RS). P2. (K1tbl) twice. K4. (K1tbl) twice. P2.

3rd row: P2. (K1tbl) twice. C4B. (K1tbl) twice. P2.

4th to 6th rows: As 1st row.

7th to 12th rows: Rep 1st to 6th rows once more.

13th row: P2. Slip next 4 sts onto cable needle and leave at back of work. K2, then knit first 2 sts from cable needle. Bring cable needle with rem 2 sts to front of work. K2, then K2 from cable needle. P2.

14th row: As 1st row.

These 14 rows form Cable Panel Pat.

With set of 4 smaller double-pointed needles, cast on 80 (86) sts. Divide sts on 3 needles. Join in rnd as (26, 26, 28) (28, 28, 30) sts, placing a marker on first st.

1st rnd: *K1. P1. Rep from * around.

Rep last rnd for 3" [7.5 cm], inc 8 (10) sts evenly across last rnd.

88 (96) sts. Place marker at end of last rnd.

Change to larger set of double-pointed needles.

1st rnd: K3 (**4**). *P1. K1tbl. Work 1st row Cable Panel pat across next 12 sts. K1tbl. P1.** K6 (**8**). Rep from * twice more, then rep from * to ** once. K3 (**4**).

Last rnd forms pat. Cable Panel Pat is now in position.

Cont in pat until work from marked rnd measures approx 4" [10 cm], ending on a 2nd row of Cable Panel.

Shape top: 1st rnd: K1 (**2**). K2tog. *P1. K1tbl. P2tog. (K1tbl) twice. C4B. (K1tbl) twice. P2tog. K1tbl. P1.** ssk. K2 (**4**). K2tog. Rep from * twice more, then rep from * to ** once. ssk. K1 (**2**). 72 (**80**) sts.

2nd to 4th rnds: K2 (**3**). *P1. K1tbl. P1. (K1tbl) twice. K4. (K1tbl) twice. P1. K1tbl. P1.** K4 (**6**). Rep from * twice more, then rep from * to ** once. K2 (**3**).

5th rnd: K0 (**1**). K2tog. *P1. K1tbl. P1. (K1tbl) twice. K4. (K1tbl) twice. P1. K1tbl. P1.** ssk. K0 (**2**). K2tog. Rep from * twice more, then rep from * to ** once. ssk. K0 (**1**). 64 (**72**) sts.

6th rnd: K1 (**2**). *P1. K1tbl. P1. (K1tbl) twice. K4. (K1tbl) twice. P1. K1tbl. P1.** K2 (**4**). Rep from * twice more, then rep from * to ** once. K1 (**2**).

7th rnd: K1 (**2**). *P1. K1tbl. P1. (K1tbl) twice. C4B. (K1tbl) twice. P1. K1tbl. P1.** K2 (**4**). Rep from * twice more, then rep from * to ** once. K1 (**2**).

8th to 10th rnds: As 6th rnd.

11th rnd: K1 (**2**). *P1. K1tbl. P1. Slip next 4 sts onto cable needle and leave at back of work. K2, then knit first 2 sts from cable needle. Bring cable needle with rem 2 sts to front of work. K2, then K2 from cable needle. P1. K1tbl. P1.** K2 (**4**). Rep from * twice more, then rep from * to ** once. K1 (**2**).

12th rnd: K1 (**2**). *P3tog. (K1tbl) twice. (K2tog) twice. (K1tbl) twice. P3tog.** K2 (**4**). Rep from * twice more, then rep from * to ** once. K1 (**2**). 40 (**48**) sts.

Size 6/12 mos only: 13th rnd: K1. *P1. (K2tog) 3 times. P1.** K2tog. Rep from * twice more, then rep from * to ** once. K1. 25 sts.

Size 18/24 mos only: 13th rnd: K2tog. *P1. (K1tbl) twice. K2tog. (K1tbl) twice. P1.** (K2tog) twice. Rep from * twice more, then rep from * to ** once. K2tog. 36 sts.

14th rnd: K1. *P1. (K1tbl) twice. K1. (K1tbl) twice. P1.** K2. Rep from * twice more, then rep from * to ** once. K1.

15th rnd: K1. *P1. K2tog. K1. K2tog. P1.** K2tog. Rep from * twice more, then rep from * to ** once. K1. 25 sts.

Both sizes: Next rnd: (K2tog) 12 times. K1. 13 sts. Break yarn, leaving a long end. Draw end tightly through rem sts. Fasten securely. BERNAT

Chart I

Start Here

Key

☐ = Knit on RS rows. Purl on WS rows.
⊟ = Purl on RS rows. Knit on WS rows.
= C4B.
🇷 = K1tbl on RS rows. P1tbl on WS rows.
= Slip next 4 sts onto cable needle and leave at back of work. K2, then knit first 2 sts from cable needle. Bring cable needle with rem 2 sts to front of work. K2, then K2 from cable needle.

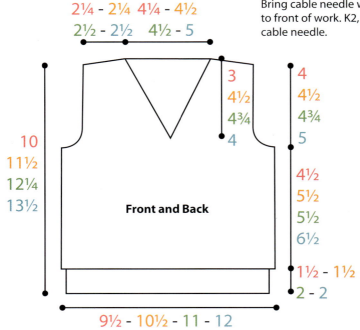

Front and Back

2¼ - 2¼   4¼ - 4½
2½ - 2½   4½ - 5

3
4½
4¾
4

4
4½
4¾
5

4½
5½
5½
6½

1½ - 1½
2 - 2

10
11½
12¼
13½

9½ - 10½ - 11 - 12

Just Dandy Set 11

2. Color Wheels Blanket

MEASUREMENTS
Blanket: Approx 37" [94 cm] square.
Motif: Approx 4½" [11.5 cm] square.

GAUGE
16 sc and 19 rows = 4" [10 cm].

MATERIALS

Bernat® Softee® Baby™ (140 g /5 oz; 331 m/362 yds)		
	Main Color (MC) (30044 Flannel)	**4 balls**
	Contrast A (30221 Soft Fern)	**1 ball**
	Contrast B (30424 Soft Red)	**1 ball**
	Contrast C (30008 Antique White)	**1 ball**
	Contrast D (30201 Aqua)	**1 ball**

Size 4 mm (U.S. G or 6) crochet hook **or size needed to obtain gauge.**

ABBREVIATIONS
See page 58 for Helpful Hints
Approx = Approximately
Beg Cluster = (Yoh and draw up a loop. Yoh and draw through 2 loops on hook) twice in same sp as last sl st. Yoh and draw through all loops on hook.
Beg = Begin(ning)
Ch(s) = Chain(s)
Cluster = (Yoh and draw up a loop. and draw through 2 loops on hook) 3 times in next ch-1 sp. Yoh and draw through all loops on hook.
Dc = Double crochet
Hdc = Half double crochet
Rep = Repeat
Rnd(s) = Round(s)
RS = Right side
Sc = Single crochet
Sl st = Slip stitch
Sp(s) = Space(s)
St(s) = Stitch(es)
Tog = Together
WS = Wrong side
Yoh = Yarn over hook

INSTRUCTIONS

MOTIF

(See Chart II on page 15).
Make 8 with MC as Color 1, C as Color 2 and B as Color 3.
Make 8 with C as Color 1, MC as Color 2 and A as Color 3.
Make 8 with A as Color 1, D as Color 2 and B as Color 3.
Make 8 with D as Color 1, A as Color 2 and C as Color 3.
Make 8 with D as Color 1, B as Color 2 and A as Color 3.
Make 8 with B as Color 1, D as Color 2 and C as Color 3.
Make 8 with MC as Color 1, A as Color 2 and D as Color 3.
Make 8 with C as Color 1, B as Color 2 and D as Color 3.

With Color 1, ch 2.
1st rnd: 6 sc in 2nd ch from hook. Join with sl st to first sc.
2nd rnd: Ch 4 (counts as dc and ch 1). 1 dc in same sp as last sl st. Ch 1. *(1 dc. Ch 1) twice in next dc. Rep from * around. Join with sl st to 3rd ch of ch 4. Fasten off.
3rd rnd: Join Color 2 with sl st to any ch-1 sp. Ch 3. Beg cluster. Ch 2. *Cluster. Ch 2. Rep from * around. Join with sl st to top of beg cluster. Fasten off.
4th rnd: Join Color 3 with sl st to any ch-2 sp. Ch 1. 3 sc in same sp as sl st. Ch 1. Miss next cluster. 3 hdc in next ch-2 sp. Ch 1. (1 dc. Ch 3. 1 dc) in top of next cluster. Ch 1. 3 hdc in next ch-2 sp. Ch 1. Miss next cluster. *3 sc in next ch-2 sp. Miss next cluster. Ch 1. 3 hdc in next ch-2 sp. Ch 1. (1 dc. Ch 3. 1 dc) in top of next cluster. Ch 1. 3 hdc in next ch-2 sp. Ch 1. Miss next cluster. Rep from * around. Join MC with sl st to first sc. Break Color 3.
5th rnd: With MC, ch 3 (counts as dc). 1 dc in each st and ch-1 sp around, working 5 dc in each corner ch-3 sp. Join with sl st to top of ch 3. Fasten off.

Join Motifs: With WS of Motifs tog and MC, crochet (sc) 8 Motifs into 8 Strips as shown in assembly diagram (see page 15). Crochet (sc) 8 strips tog, working ch 1 over ridge from previous sc seam.

BORDER

With RS facing, join MC with sl st to any corner dc of Blanket.
1st rnd: Ch 3 (counts as dc). 4 dc in same sp as sl st. 1 dc in each dc and side of sc (seams) around, working 5 dc in each corner. Join C with sl st to top of ch 3. Break MC.
2nd rnd: With C, ch 1. *Working from **left** to right instead of **right** to left as usual,* work 1 reverse sc in each dc around. Join with sl st to first sc. Fasten off. BERNAT

Reverse Sc

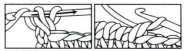

Chart II

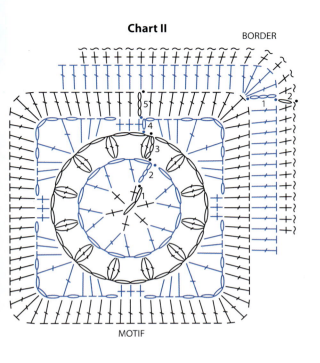

Key

◯ = chain (ch)
• = slip st (sl st)
+ = single crochet (sc)
~ = reverse single crochet (reverse sc)
T = half double crochet (hdc)
+ = double crochet (dc)
◊ = beginning cluster (beg cluster)
◊ = cluster

Diagram

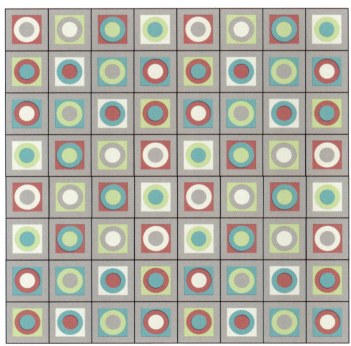

Color Wheels Blanket

3. Swirly Skirt

SIZES

To fit waist measurement	
6 mos	17" [43 cm]
12 mos	18" [45.5 cm]
18 mos	19" [48 cm]
24 mos	20" [51 cm]

MATERIALS

Bernat® Softee® Baby™ (140 g /5 oz; 331 m/362 yds)						
	Sizes	6	12	18	24	mos
	Main Color (MC) (30201 Aqua)	1	1	1	1	**ball**
	Contrast A (02004 Mint)	1	1	1	1	**ball**
	Contrast B (30424 Soft Red)	1	1	1	1	**ball**
Size 4 mm (U.S. G or 6) crochet hook **or size needed to obtain gauge.** Length of ¾" [2 cm] wide elastic.						

GAUGE

16 sc and 19 rows = 4" [10 cm].

ABBREVIATIONS

See page 58 for Helpful Hints.

Beg = Beginning

Beg Cluster = Ch 2. (Yoh and draw up a loop. Yoh and draw through 2 loops on hook) twice in same st. Yoh and draw through all loops on hook

Ch(s) = Chain(s)

Cluster = (Yoh and draw up a loop. Yoh and draw through 2 loops on hook) 3 times in same st. Yoh and draw through all loops on hook

Dc = Double crochet

Dc3tog = (Yoh and draw up a loop in next st. Yoh and draw through 2 loops on hook) 3 times. Yoh and draw through all loops on hook

Hdc = Half double crochet

Rep = Repeat

Rnd(s) = Round(s)

Sc = Single crochet

Sc3tog = Draw up a loop in each of next 3 sts. Yoh and draw through all loops on hook

Sl st = Slip stitch

Sp(s) = Space(s)

St(s) = Stitch(es)

Tog = Together

Tr = Treble crochet

WS = Wrong side

Yoh = Yarn over hook

INSTRUCTIONS

The instructions are written for smallest size. If changes are necessary for larger sizes the instructions will be written thus ( ). Numbers for each size are shown in the same color throughout the pattern. When only one number is given in black, it applies to all sizes.

Note: When joining colors, work to last 2 loops on hook of first color. Draw new color through last 2 loops then proceed. Ch 3 at beg of rnd counts as dc.

Waistband: With MC, ch **76** (**80**-**84**-**88**). Join with sl st to first ch to form a ring, taking care not to twist ch.

1st rnd: Ch 1. 1 sc in each ch around. Join with sl st to first sc. **76** (**80**-**84**-**88**) sc.

2nd rnd: Ch 3. 1 dc in each sc around. Join with sl st to top of ch 3.

3rd rnd: Ch 1. 1 sc in each dc around. Join with sl st to first sc.

4th to 7th rnds: Rep 2nd and 3rd rnds twice more.

Skirt: 1st rnd: With MC, ch 1. (1 sc in next sc. 1 hdc in next sc. 3 dc in next sc. 1 hdc in next sc) **19** (**20**-**21**-**22**) times. Join with sl st to first sc. **114** (**120**-**126**-**132**) sts.
(See Chart III on page 23).

2nd rnd: Sl st in each of first 3 sts. Ch 3. 3 tr in next dc. 1 dc in next dc. Dc3tog. (1 dc in next dc. 3 tr in next dc. 1 dc in next dc. Dc3tog) **18** (**19**-**20**-**21**) times. Join with sl st to top of ch 3. Fasten off.

3rd rnd: Join A with sl st to center tr of any 3-tr group. Ch 1. 3 sc in same sp as sl st. 2 sc in next tr. Sc3tog. 2 sc in next tr. (3 sc in next tr. 2 sc in next tr. Sc3tog. 2 sc in next tr) **18** (**19**-**20**-**21**) times. Join with sl st to first sc. Fasten off.

4th rnd: Join B with sl st to center sc of any 3-sc group. (Beg cluster. Ch 1. Cluster) in same sp as sl st. (Ch 1. Miss next sc. Cluster in next sc) 3 times. Ch 1. Miss next sc. [(Cluster. Ch 1. Cluster) in next sc. (Ch 1. Miss next sc. Cluster in next sc) 3 times. Ch 1. Miss next sc] **18** (**19**-**20**-**21**) times. Join with sl st to first cluster. Fasten off.

Swirly Skirt 17

5th rnd: Join A with sl st to any ch-1 sp between 2-cluster groups. Ch 1. 3 sc in same sp as sl st. 1 sc in each of next 3 sts. Sc3tog. 1 sc in each of next 3 sts. (3 sc in next st. 1 sc in each of next 3 sts. Sc3tog. 1 sc in each of next 3 sts) **18** (**19**-**20**-**21**) times. Join with sl st to first sc. Fasten off.

6th rnd: Join MC with sl st in center sc of any 3-sc group. Ch 3. 2 dc in same sp as sl st. 1 dc in each of next 3 sc. Dc3tog. 1 dc in each of next 3 dc. (3 dc in next sc. 1 dc in each of next 3 sc. Dc3tog. 1 dc in each of next 3 dc) **18** (**19**-**20**-**21**) times. Join with sl st to top of ch 3.

7th rnd: Ch 1. 1 sc in first dc. (3 sc in next dc. 1 sc in each of next 3 dc. Sc3tog. 1 sc in each of next 3 dc) **18** (**19**-**20**-**21**) times. 3 sc in next dc. 1 sc in each of next 3 dc. Sc3tog. 1 sc in each of next 2 dc. Join with sl st to first sc.

8th rnd: Ch 3. 1 dc in next sc. (3 dc in next sc. 1 dc in each of next 3 sc. Dc3tog. 1 dc in each of next 3 sc) **18** (**19**-**20**-**21**) times. 3 dc in next sc. 1 dc in each of next 3 sc. Dc3tog. 1 dc in next sc. Join with sl st to top of ch 3. Fasten off.

9th rnd: Join A with sl st to center dc of any 3-dc group. Ch 1. 3 sc in same dc. 2 sc in next dc. 1 sc in each of next 2 dc. Sc3tog. 1 sc in each of next 2 dc. 2 sc in next dc. (3 sc in next dc. 2 sc in next dc. 1 sc in each of next 2 dc. Sc3tog. 1 sc in each of next 2 dc. 2 sc in next dc) **18** (**19**-**20**-**21**) times. Join with sl st to first sc. Fasten off.

10th rnd: Join B with sl st to center sc of any 3-sc group. (Beg cluster. Ch 1. Cluster) in same sp as sl st. (Ch 1. Miss next sc. Cluster in next sc) 5 times. Ch 1. Miss next sc. [(Cluster. Ch 1. Cluster) in next sc. (Ch 1. Miss next sc. Cluster in next sc) 5 times. Ch 1. Miss next sc] **18** (**19**-**20**-**21**) times. Join with sl st to first cluster. Fasten off.

11th rnd: Join A with sl st to any ch-1 sp between 2-cluster groups. Ch 1. 3 sc in same sp as sl st. 1 sc in each of next 5 sts. Sc3tog. 1 sc in each of next 5 sts. (3 sc in next st. 1 sc in each of next 5 sts. Sc3tog. 1 sc in each of next 5 sts) **18** (**19**-**20**-**21**) times. Join with sl st to first sc. Fasten off.

12th rnd: Join MC with sl st to center sc of any 3-sc group. Ch 3. 2 dc in same sp as sl st. 1 dc in each of next 5 sc. Dc3tog. 1 dc in each of next 5 sc. (3 dc in next sc. 1 dc in each of next 5 sc. Dc3tog. 1 dc in each of next 5 sc) **18** (**19**-**20**-**21**) times. Join with sl st to top of ch 3.

13th rnd: Ch 1. 1 sc in first dc. (3 sc in next dc. 1 sc in each of next 5 dc. Sc3tog. 1 sc in each of next 5 dc) **18** (**19**-**20**-**21**) times. 3 sc in next dc. 1 sc in each of next 5 dc. Sc3tog. 1 sc in each of next 4 dc. Join with sl st to first sc.

14th rnd: Ch 3. 1 dc in next sc. (3 dc in next sc. 1 dc in each of next 5 sc. Dc3tog. 1 dc in each of next 5 sc) **18** (**19**-**20**-**21**) times. 3 sc in next dc. 1 sc in each of next 5 sc. Dc3tog. 1 dc in each of next 3 sc. Join with sl st to top of ch 3. Fasten off.

15th rnd: Join A with sl st to center dc of any 3-dc group. Ch 1. 3 sc in same sp as sl st. 2 sc in next dc. 1 sc in each of next 4 dc. Sc3tog. 1 sc in each of next 4 dc. 2 sc in next dc. (3 sc in next dc. 2 sc in next dc. 1 sc in each of next 4 dc. Sc3tog. 1 sc in each of next 4 dc. 2 sc in next dc) **18** (**19**-**20**-**21**) times. Join with sl st to first sc. Fasten off.

16th rnd: Join B with sl st to center sc of any 3-sc group. (Beg cluster. Ch 1. Cluster) in same sp as sl st. (Ch 1. Miss next sc. Cluster in next sc) 7 times. Ch 1. Miss next sc. [(Cluster. Ch 1. Cluster) in next sc. (Ch 1. Miss next sc. Cluster in next sc) 7 times. Ch 1. Miss next sc] **18** (**19**-**20**-**21**) times. Join with sl st to first cluster. Fasten off.

17th rnd: Join A with sl st to any ch-1 sp between 2-cluster groups. Ch 1. 3 sc in same sp as sl st. 1 sc in each of next 7 sts. Sc3tog. 1 sc in each of next 7 sts. (3 sc in next st. 1 sc in each of next 7 sts. Sc3tog. 1 sc in each of next 7 sts) **18** (**19**-**20**-**21**) times. Join with sl st to first sc. Fasten off.

18th rnd: Join MC with sl st to center sc of any 3-sc group. Ch 3. 2 dc in same sp as sl st. 1 dc in each of next 7 sc. Dc3tog. 1 dc in each of next 7 sc. (3 dc in next sc. 1 dc in each of next 7 sc. Dc3tog. 1 dc in each of next 7 sc) **18** (**19**-**20**-**21**) times. Join with sl st to top of ch 3.

19th rnd: Ch 1. 1 sc in first dc. (3 sc in next dc. 1 sc in each of next 7 dc. Sc3tog. 1 sc in each of next 7 dc) **18** (**19**-**20**-**21**) times. 3 sc in next dc. 1 sc in each of next 7 dc. Sc3tog. 1 sc in each of next 6 dc. Join with sl st to first sc.

Size **6 mos only:** Fasten off.

Sizes **12**, **18** and **24** mos only: **20th rnd:** Ch 3. 1 dc in next sc. (3 dc in next sc. 1 dc in each of next 7 sc. Dc3tog. 1 dc in each of next 7 sc) (**19**-**20**-**21**) times. 3 dc in next sc. 1 dc in each of next 7 sc. Dc3tog. 1 dc in each of next 5 sc. Join with sl st to top of ch 3. Fasten off.

21st rnd: Join A with sl st to center dc of any 3-dc group. Ch 1. 3 sc in same sp as sl st. 2 sc in next dc. 1 sc in each of next 6 dc. Sc3tog. 1 sc in each of next 6 dc. 2 sc in next dc. (3 sc in next dc. 2 sc in next dc. 1 sc in each of next 6 dc. Sc3tog. 1 sc in each of next 6 dc. 2 sc in next dc) (**19**-**20**-**21**) times. Join with sl st to first sc. Fasten off.

22nd rnd: Join B with sl st to center sc of any 3-sc group. (Beg cluster. Ch 1. Cluster) in same sl as sl st. (Ch 1. Miss next sc. Cluster in next sc) 9 times. Ch 1. Miss next sc. [(Cluster. Ch 1. Cluster) in next sc. (Ch 1. Miss next sc. Cluster in next sc) 9 times. Ch 1. Miss next sc] (**19**-**20**-**21**) times. Join with sl st to first cluster. Fasten off.

23rd rnd: Join A with sl st to any ch-1 sp between 2-cluster groups. Ch 1. 3 sc in same sp as sl st. 1 sc in each of next 9 sts. Sc3tog. 1 sc in each of next 9 sts. (3 sc in next st. 1 sc in each of next 9 sts. Sc3tog. 1 sc in each of next 9 sts) (**19**-**20**-**21**) times. Join with sl st to first sc. Fasten off.

24th rnd: Join MC with sl st in center sc of any 3-sc group. Ch 3. 2 dc in same sp as sl st. 1 dc in each of next 9 sc. Dc3tog. 1 dc in each of next 9 sc. (3 dc in next sc. 1 dc in each of next 9 sc. Dc3tog. 1 dc in each of next 9 sc) (**19**-**20**-**21**) times. Join with sl st to top of ch 3.

25th rnd: Ch 1. 1 sc in first dc. (3 sc in next dc. 1 sc in each of next 9 dc. Sc3tog. 1 sc in each of next 9 dc) (**19**-**20**-**21**) times. 3 sc in next dc. 1 sc in each of next 9 dc. Sc3tog. 1 sc in each of next 8 dc. Join with sl st to first sc.

Size 12 mos only: Fasten off.

Sizes 18 and 24 mos only: 26th rnd: Ch 3. 1 dc in next sc. (3 dc in next sc. 1 dc in each of next 9 sc. Dc3tog. 1 dc in each of next 9 sc) (**20**-**21**) times. 3 sc in next dc. 1 dc in each of next 9 sc. Dc3tog. 1 dc in each of next 7 sc. Join with sl st to top of ch 3. Fasten off.

27th rnd: Join A with sl st to center dc of any 3-dc group. Ch 1. 3 sc in same sp as sl st. 2 sc in next dc. 1 sc in each of next 8 dc. Sc3tog. 1 sc in each of next 8 dc. 2 sc in next dc. (3 sc in next dc. 2 sc in next dc. 1 sc in each of next 8 dc. Sc3tog. 1 sc in each of next 8 dc. 2 sc in next dc) (**20**-**21**) times. Join with sl st to first sc. Fasten off.

28th rnd: Join B with sl st to center sc of any 3-sc group. (Beg cluster. Ch 1. Cluster) in same sp as sl st. (Ch 1. Miss next sc. Cluster in next sc) 11 times. Ch 1. Miss next sc. [(Cluster. Ch 1. Cluster) in next sc. (Ch 1. Miss next sc. Cluster in next sc) 11 times. Ch 1. Miss next sc] (**20**-**21**) times. Join with sl st to first cluster. Fasten off.

29th rnd: Join A with sl st to any ch-1 sp between 2-cluster groups. Ch 1. 3 sc in same sp as sl st. 1 sc in each of next 11 sts. Sc3tog. 1 sc in each of next 11 sts. (3 sc in next st. 1 sc in each of next 11 sts. Sc3tog. 1 sc in each of next 11 sts) (**20**-**21**) times. Join with sl st to first sc. Fasten off.

30th rnd: Join MC with sl st in center sc of any 3-sc group. Ch 3. 2 dc in same sp as last sl st. 1 dc in each of next 11 sc. Dc3tog. 1 dc in each of next 11 sc. (3 dc in next sc. 1 dc in each of next 11 sc. Dc3tog. 1 dc in each of next 11 sc) (**20**-**21**) times. Join with sl st to top of ch 3.

31st rnd: Ch 1. 1 sc in first dc. (3 sc in next dc. 1 sc in each of next 11 dc. Sc3tog. 1 sc in each of next 11 dc) (**20**-**21**) times. 3 sc in next dc. 1 sc in each of next 11 dc. Sc3tog. 1 sc in each of next 10 dc. Join with sl st to first sc.

Size 18 mos only: Fasten off.

Size 24 mos only: 32nd rnd: Ch 3. 1 dc in next sc. (3 dc in next sc. 1 dc in each of next 11 sc. Dc3tog. 1 dc in each of next 11 sc) 21 times. 3 sc in next dc. 1 sc in each of next 11 sc. Dc3tog. 1 dc in each of next 9 sc. Join with sl st to top of ch 3. Fasten off.

33rd rnd: Join A with sl st to center dc of any 3-dc group. Ch 1. 3 sc in same sp as sl st. 2 sc in next dc. 1 sc in each of next 10 dc. Sc3tog. 1 sc in each of next 10 dc. 2 sc in next dc. (3 sc in next dc. 2 sc in next dc. 1 sc in each of next 10 dc. Sc3tog. 1 sc in each of next 10 dc. 2 sc in next dc) 21 times. Join with sl st to first sc. Fasten off.

34th rnd: Join B with sl st to center sc of any 3-sc group. (Beg cluster. Ch 1. Cluster) in same sp as sl st. (Ch 1. Miss next sc. Cluster in next sc) 13 times. Ch 1. Miss next sc. [(Cluster. Ch 1. Cluster) in next sc. (Ch 1. Miss next sc. Cluster in next sc) 13 times. Ch 1. Miss next sc] 21 times. Join with sl st to first cluster. Fasten off.

35th rnd: Join A with sl st to any ch-1 sp between 2-cluster groups. Ch 1. 3 sc in same sp as sl st. 1 sc in each of next 13 sts. Sc3tog. 1 sc in each of next 13 sts. (3 sc in next st. 1 sc in each of next 13 sts. Sc3tog. 1 sc in each of next 13 sts) 21 times. Join with sl st to first sc. Fasten off.

36th rnd: Join MC with sl st to center sc of any 3-sc group. Ch 3. 2 dc in same sp as sl st. 1 dc in each of next 13 sc. Dc3tog. 1 dc in each of next 13 sc. (3 dc in next sc. 1 dc in each of next 13 sc. Dc3tog. 1 dc in each of next 13 sc) 21 times. Join with sl st to top of ch 3.

37th rnd: Ch 1. 1 sc in first dc. (3 sc in next dc. 1 sc in each of next 13 dc. Sc3tog. 1 sc in each of next 13 dc) 21 times. 3 sc in next dc. 1 sc in each of next 13 dc. Sc3tog. 1 sc in each of next 12 dc. Join with sl st to first sc. Fasten off.

FINISHING

Fold waistband to WS and sew along last rnd of waistband in position for casing, leaving an opening to insert elastic. Cut elastic to fit waist measurement. Insert through waistband and sew ends of elastic tog securely. Sew waistband opening closed.

Bow: With B, ch 40. Fasten off. Tie into bow and sew to center front of Waistband.

BERNAT

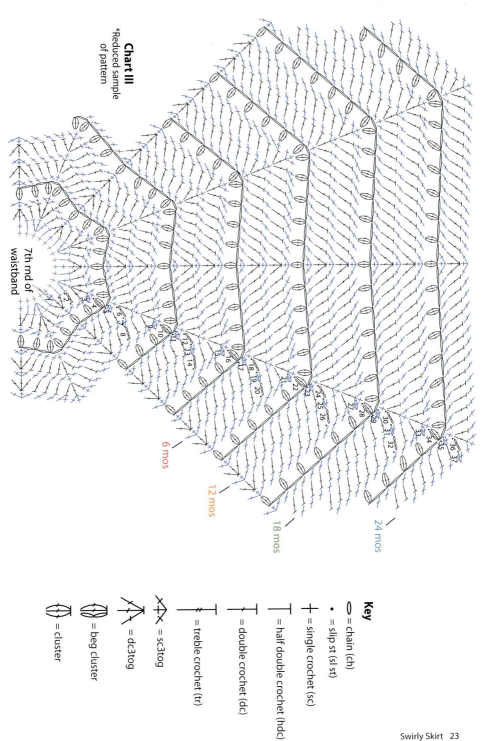

4. Sitting Pretty Set

 CIRCULAR NEEDLE   DOUBLE-POINTED NEEDLES   LIGHT   INTERMEDIATE

SIZES
Jumper Dress

To fit chest measurement	
6 mos	17" [43 cm]
12 mos	18" [45.5 cm]
18 mos	19" [48 cm]
24 mos	20" [51 cm]

Finished chest	
6 mos	18" [45.5 cm]
12 mos	19" [48 cm]
18 mos	21" [53.5 cm]
24 mos	22" [56 cm]

Hat: To fit 6/12 (18/24) mos

MATERIALS

Bernat® Softee® Baby™ (140 g /5 oz; 331 m/362 yds)						
Jumper Dress	**Sizes**	6	12	18	24	mos
30424 (Soft Red)		1	2	2	2	ball(s)

Sizes 3.5 mm (U.S. 4) and 4 mm (U.S. 6) circular knitting needles 24" [60.5 cm] long. Set of four size 3.5 mm (U.S. 4) double-pointed knitting needles **or size needed to obtain gauge.** Cable needle. 3 buttons. 1 stitch holder.

Hat	**Sizes**	6/12	18/24	mos
30424 (Soft Red)		1	1	ball

Set of four sizes 3.5 mm (U.S. 4) and 4 mm (U.S. 6) double-pointed knitting needles **or size needed to obtain gauge.** Cable needle.

ABBREVIATIONS

See page 58 for Helpful Hints.

2tog = K2tog or P2tog as appropriate
Alt = Alternate(ing)
Approx = Approximately
Beg = Beginning
C4B = Slip next 2 stitches onto cable needle and leave at back of work. K2, then K2 from cable needle
Cont = Continue(ity)
Dec = Decrease(ing)
Inc = Increase 1 stitch by knitting into front and back of next stitch
K = Knit
K1tbl = Knit next stitch through back of loop
K2tog = Knit next 2 stitches together
P = Purl
Pat = Pattern
P2(3)tog = Purl next 2 (3) stitches together
P2togtbl = Purl next 2 stitches through back loops
P1tbl = Purl next stitch through back of loop
Pat = Pattern
Rem = Remaining
Rep = Repeat
Rnd(s) = Round(s)
RS = Right side
St(s) = Stitch(es)
Ssk = Slip next 2 stitches knitwise one at a time. Pass them back onto left-hand needle, then knit through back loops together
WS = Wrong side

GAUGE

22 sts and 30 rows = 4" [10 cm] in stocking st with larger needles.

INSTRUCTIONS

Cable Panel (worked over 12 sts in **rnds**). (See Chart IV on page 32).
1st and 2nd rows: (RS). P2. (K1tbl) twice. K4. (K1tbl) twice. P2.
3rd row: P2. (K1tbl) twice. C4B. (K1tbl) twice. P2.
4th to 6th rows: As 1st row.
7th to 12th rows: Rep 1st to 6th rows once more.
13th row: P2. Slip next 4 sts onto cable needle and leave at back of work. K2, then knit first 2 sts from cable needle. Bring cable needle with rem 2 sts to front of work. K2, then K2 from cable needle. P2.
14th row: As 1st row.
These 14 rows form Cable Panel Pat.

JUMPER DRESS

The instructions are written for smallest size. If changes are necessary for larger sizes the instructions will be written thus ( ). Numbers for each size are shown in the same color throughout the pattern. When only one number is given in black, it applies to all sizes.

Note: Dress is worked in one piece to placket opening. Refer to Cable Panel Pat worked in rnds until Dress is divided and worked back and forth in rows. At that time, refer to Cable Panel Pat worked in rows.

SKIRT

With smaller circular needle cast on **160** (**168**-**184**-**200**) sts. Join in rnd, placing a marker on first st.
1st rnd: Purl.
2nd rnd: Knit.
Rep last 2 rnds 4 times more, inc 8 sts evenly around last rnd. **168** (**176**-**192**-**208**) sts.

Change to larger needle and proceed in pat as follows:

1st rnd: K**8** (**8**-**12**-**14**). *P1. K1tbl. Work 1st row Cable Panel Pat across next 12 sts. K1tbl. P1.* K**36** (**40**-**40**-**44**). Rep from * to * once more. K**16** (**16**-**24**-**28**). Rep from * to * once more. K**36** (**40**-**40**-**44**). Rep from * to * once more. K**8** (**8**-**12**-**14**).

Last rnd forms pat. Cable Panel Pat is now in position.

Cont in pat until work from beg measures approx 8¾ (8¾-10½-10½)" [**22** (**22**-**26.5**-**26.5**) cm], ending with a 14th row of Cable Panel Pat.

Bodice: Dec rnd: (P2tog) **4** (**4**-**6**-**7**) times. *P1. K1tbl. Work 1st row Cable Panel Pat across next 12 sts. K1tbl. P1.* (P2tog) **18** (**20**-**20**-**22**) times. Rep from * to * once more. (P2tog) **8** (**8**-**12**-**14**) times. Rep from * to * once more. (P2tog) **18** (**20**-**20**-**22**) times. Rep from * to * once more. (P2tog) **4** (**4**-**6**-**7**) times. **116** (**120**-**128**-**136**) sts. Place marker on last rnd.

Cable Panel (worked over 12 sts in **rows**).
1st row: (RS). P2. (K1tbl) twice. K4. (K1tbl) twice. P2.
2nd and alt rows: K2. (P1tbl) twice. P4. (P1tbl) twice. K2.
3rd row: P2. (K1tbl) twice. C4B. (K1tbl) twice. P2.
5th row: As 1st row.
6th row: As 2nd row.
7th to 12th rows: Rep 1st to 6th rows once more.

13th row: P2. Slip next 4 sts onto cable needle and leave at back of work. K2, then knit first 2 sts from cable needle. Bring cable needle with rem 2 sts to front of work. K2, then K2 from cable needle. P2.
14th row: As 2nd row.
These 14 rows form Cable Panel Pat.

Divide for Front placket opening: Turn work so WS is now facing and cont in rows (following Cable Panel Pat worked in rows) as follows:
Next row: (WS). P**4** (**4**-**6**-**7**). *K1. P1tbl. Work 2nd row Cable Panel Pat across next 12 sts. P1tbl. K1.* P**18** (**20**-**20**-**22**). Rep from * to * once more. P**8** (**8**-**12**-**14**). Rep from * to * once more. P**6** (**7**-**7**-**8**). Cast off next 6 sts (center Front). P**6** (**7**-**7**-**8**). Rep from * to * once more. P**4** (**4**-**6**-**7**). Break yarn.

Rearrange sts as follows: Slip last **26** (**27**-**29**-**31**) sts worked back onto left-hand side of circular needle. **Turn work so RS is now facing** and cont in rows (following Cable Panel Pat worked in rows) as follows:
Next row: (RS). Rejoin yarn to first st after center Front cast off. K**6** (**7**-**7**-**8**). *P1. K1tbl. Work 3rd row Cable Panel Pat across next 12 sts. K1tbl. P1.* K**8** (**8**-**12**-**14**). Rep from * to * once more. K**18** (**20**-**20**-**22**). Rep from * to * once more. K**8** (**8**-**12**-**14**). Rep from * to * once more. K**6** (**7**-**7**-**8**). **110** (**114**-**122**-**130**) sts.
Next row: P**6** (**7**-**7**-**8**). *K1. P1tbl. Work 4th row Cable Panel Pat across next 12 sts. P1tbl. K1.* P**8** (**8**-**12**-**14**). Rep from * to * once more. P**18** (**20**-**20**-**22**). Rep from * to * once more. P**8** (**8**-**12**-**14**). Rep from * to * once more. P**6** (**7**-**7**-**8**).

Cont in pat (working in rows) until work from marked rnd measures 2 (2½-2½-3)" [5 (6-6-7.5) cm], ending with a WS row.

Shape armholes: Next row: (RS). K6 (7-7-8). *P1. K1tbl. Work appropriate row Cable Panel Pat across next 12 sts. K1tbl. P1.* K1. Cast off 6 (6-10-12) sts. K1. Rep from * to * once more. K18 (20-20-22). Rep from * to * once more. K1. Cast off 6 (6-10-12) sts. K1. Rep from * to * once more. K6 (7-7-8).

Rearrange sts as follows: Slip last 23 (24-24-25) sts worked back onto left-hand side of circular needle. **Turn work so WS is now facing** and cont in rows (following Cable Panel Pat worked in rows) as follows:

Back Bodice: With WS facing, rejoin yarn to first st after armhole cast off. P1. *K1. P1tbl. Work appropriate row Cable Panel Pat across next 12 sts. P1tbl. K1.* P18 (20-20-22). Rep from * to * once more. P1. 52 (54-54-56) sts. Cont in pat, dec 1 st at armhole edge on next and every following alt row twice more. 46 (48-48-50) sts.
Cont even in pat until armhole measures 2½ (3-3¼-3½)" [6 (7.5-8.5-9) cm], ending with a WS row.

Shape back neck: Next row: (RS). Pat across 18 sts (neck edge). **Turn.** Leave rem sts on a spare needle.
Keeping cont of pat, dec 1 st at neck edge on next 4 rows, then on every following alt row twice more. 12 sts.
Work 1 row even in pat. Cast off.

With RS facing, slip next 10 (12-12-14) sts onto a st holder. Join yarn to rem sts and pat to end of row.
Keeping cont of pat, dec 1 st at neck edge on next 4 rows, then on every following alt row twice more. 12 sts.
Work 1 row even in pat. Cast off.

Left Front Bodice: With WS facing, rejoin yarn at center Front. P6 (7-7-8). K1. P1tbl. Work appropriate row Cable Panel Pat across next 12 sts. P1tbl. K1. P1. 23 (24-24-25) sts.
Keeping cont of pat, dec 1 st at armhole edge on next and every following alt row twice more. 20 (21-21-22) sts.
Work 2 rows even in pat.

Shape neck: Next row: (WS). Cast off 3 sts. Pat to end of row.
Keeping cont of pat, dec 1 st at neck edge on next row and following alt row, then on every following 4th row until 12 sts rem.
Cont even in pat until armhole measures same length as Back Bodice, ending with a WS row. Cast off.

Right Front Bodice: With WS facing, rejoin yarn at armhole edge of Right Front. P1. K1. P1tbl. Work appropriate row Cable Panel Pat across next 12 sts. P1tbl. K1. P6 (7-7-8). 23 (24-24-25) sts.
Keeping cont of pat, dec 1 st at armhole edge on next and every following alt row twice more. 20 (21-21-22) sts.
Work 1 row even in pat.

Shape neck: Next row: (RS). Cast off 3 sts. Pat to end of row.

Work 1 row even in pat.

Keeping cont of pat, dec 1 st at neck edge on next and following alt row, then on every following 4th row until 12 sts rem. Cont even in pat until armhole measures same length as Back Bodice, ending with a WS row. Cast off.

FINISHING

Pin pieces to measurements. Cover with a damp cloth leaving cloth to dry. Sew shoulder seams.

Armbands: With RS facing and set of double-pointed needles, beg at center of armhole cast off edge, pick up and knit **58** (**62**-**70**-**78**) sts evenly around armhole edge. Divide sts onto 3 needles. Join in rnd, placing a marker on first st.

1st rnd: *K1. P1. Rep from * around.

Rep last rnd of (K1. P1) ribbing 3 times more. Cast off in ribbing.

Neckband: With RS facing and smaller circular needle, pick up and knit **20** (**22**-**25**-**27**) sts up Right Front neck edge and 9 sts down Right Back neck edge. K**10** (**12**-**12**-**14**) from Back st holder, inc 1 st at center. Pick up and knit 9 sts up Left Back neck edge and **20** (**22**-**25**-**27**) sts down Left Front neck edge. **69** (**75**-**81**-**87**) sts. **Do not** join. Working back and forth across needle in rows, proceed as follows:

1st row: (WS). *P1. K1. Rep from * to last st. P1.
2nd row: *K1. P1. Rep from * to last st. K1.
Rep last 2 rows of (K1. P1) ribbing once more. Cast off in ribbing.

Placket Buttonhole Band: With RS facing and smaller circular needle, pick up and knit **20** (**22**-**22**-**24**) sts up Right Front placket opening to edge of neckband.

1st row: (WS). *P1. K1. Rep from * to end of row.

2nd row: *P1. K1. Rep from * to end of row.

3rd row: As 1st row.

4th row: Rib across 3 sts. [Cast off 2 sts. Rib across **4** (**5**-**5**-**6**) sts] twice. Cast off 2 sts. Rib 3 sts.

5th row: Rib, casting on 2 sts over cast off sts.

6th row: As 2nd row.

7th and 8th rows As 1st and 2nd rows. Cast off in ribbing.

Placket Button Band: With RS facing and smaller circular needle, pick up and knit **20** (**22**-**22**-**24**) sts down Left Front placket opening between edge of neckband and placket edge.

Work 8 rows in (K1. P1) ribbing as given for Buttonhole band, omitting references to buttonholes. Cast off in ribbing.

Sew sides of Placket Bands to cast off sts at center Front, lapping Buttonhole Band over Button Band. Sew buttons in position to correspond to buttonholes.

HAT

The instructions are written for smaller size. If changes are necessary for larger size the instructions will be written thus ( ). Numbers for each size are shown in the same color throughout the pattern. When only one number is given in black, it applies to both sizes.

Cable Panel (worked over 12 sts in **rnds**). (See Chart IV on page 32).

1st and 2nd rows: (RS). P2. (K1tbl) twice. K4. (K1tbl) twice. P2.

3rd row: P2. (K1tbl) twice. C4B. (K1tbl) twice. P2.

4th to 6th rows: As 1st row.

7th to 12th rows: Rep 1st to 6th rows once more.

13th row: P2. Slip next 4 sts onto cable needle and leave at back of work. K2, then knit first 2 sts from cable needle. Bring cable needle with rem 2 sts to front of work. K2, then K2 from cable needle. P2.

14th row: As 1st row.

These 14 rows form Cable Panel Pat.

With set of 4 smaller double-pointed needles, cast on **80** (**86**) sts. Divide sts on 3 needles. Join in rnd, placing a marker on first st.

1st rnd: *K1. P1. Rep from * around.

Rep last rnd of (K1. P1) ribbing for 3½" [9 cm] inc **8** (**10**) sts evenly across last rnd. **88** (**96**) sts. Place markers at each end of last rnd.

Change to larger set of double-pointed needles.

1st rnd: K**3** (**4**). *P1. K1tbl. Work 1st row Cable Panel Pat across next 12 sts. K1tbl. P1.** K**6** (**8**). Rep from * twice more, then rep from * to ** once. K**3** (**4**).

Last rnd forms pat. Cable Panel pat is now in position.

Cont in Pat until work from marked rnd measures approx 4" [10 cm], ending on a 2nd row of Cable Panel Pat.

Shape top: 1st rnd: K**1** (**2**). K2tog. *P1. K1tbl. P2tog. (K1tbl) twice. C4B. (K1tbl) twice. P2tog. K1tbl. P1.** ssk. K**2** (**4**). K2tog. Rep from * twice more, then rep from * to ** once. ssk. K**1** (**2**). **72** (**80**) sts.

2nd to 4th rnds: K**2** (**3**). *P1. K1tbl. P1. (K1tbl) twice. K4. (K1tbl) twice. P1. K1tbl. P1.** K**4** (**6**). Rep from * twice more, then rep from * to ** once. K**2** (**3**).

5th rnd: K**0** (**1**). K2tog. *P1. K1tbl. P1. (K1tbl) twice. K4. (K1tbl) twice. P1. K1tbl. P1.** ssk. K**0** (**2**). K2tog. Rep from * twice more, then rep from * to ** once. ssk. K**0** (**1**). **64** (**72**) sts.

6th rnd: K**1** (**2**). *P1. K1tbl. P1. (K1tbl) twice. K4. (K1tbl) twice. P1. K1tbl. P1.** K**2** (**4**). Rep from * twice more, then rep from * to ** once. K**1** (**2**).

7th rnd: K**1** (**2**). *P1. K1tbl. P1. (K1tbl) twice. C4B. (K1tbl) twice. P1. K1tbl. P1.** K**2** (**4**). Rep from * twice more, then rep from * to ** once. K**1** (**2**).

8th to 10th rnds: As 6th rnd.

11th rnd: K**1** (**2**). *P1. K1tbl. P1. Slip next 4 sts onto cable needle and leave at back of work. K2, then knit first 2 sts from cable needle. Bring cable needle with rem 2 sts to front of work. K2, then K2 from cable needle. P1. K1tbl. P1.** K**2** (**4**). Rep from * twice more, then rep from * to ** once. K**1** (**2**).

12th rnd: K**1** (**2**). *P3tog. (K1tbl) twice. (K2tog) twice. (K1tbl) twice. P3tog.** K**2** (**4**). Rep from * twice more, then rep from * to ** once. K**1** (**2**). **40** (**48**) sts.

Size 6/12 mos only: 13th rnd: K1. *P1. (K2tog) 3 times. P1.** K2tog. Rep from * twice more, then rep from * to ** once. K1. 25 sts.

Size 18/24 mos only: 13th rnd: K2tog. *P1. (K1tbl) twice. K2tog. (K1tbl) twice. P1.** (K2tog) twice. Rep from * twice more, then rep from * to ** once. K2tog. 36 sts.

14th rnd: K1. *P1. (K1tbl) twice. K1. (K1tbl) twice. P1.** K2. Rep from * twice more, then rep from * to ** once. K1.

15th rnd: K1. *P1. K2tog. K1. K2tog. P1.** K2tog. Rep from * twice more, then rep from * to ** once. K1. 25 sts.

Both sizes: Next rnd: (K2tog) 12 times. K1. 13 sts. Break yarn, leaving a long end. Draw end tightly through rem sts.

Pom-pom: Wind yarn around 3 fingers approx 60 times. Remove from fingers and tie tightly in center. Cut through each side of loops. Trim to a smooth round shape. Sew pom-pom to top of Hat. **BERNAT**

Chart IV

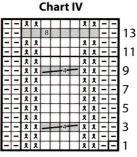

Start Here

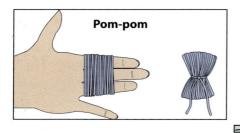

Pom-pom

Key

☐ = Knit
⊟ = Purl
▭▭▭ = C4B.
🇽 = K1tbl
▭▭▭▭▭▭▭▭ = Slip next 4 sts onto cable needle and leave at back of work. K2, then knit first 2 sts from cable needle. Bring cable needle with rem 2 sts to front of work. K2, then K2 from cable needle.

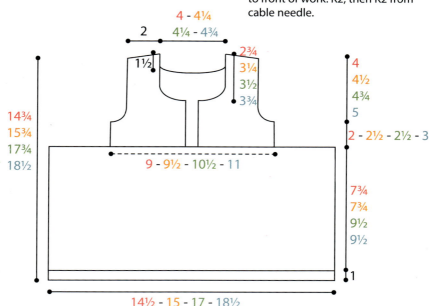

5. Playtime Set

 LIGHT | **INTERMEDIATE**

SIZES
Cardigan

To fit chest measurement	
6 mos	17" [43 cm]
12 mos	18" [45.5 cm]
18 mos	19" [48 cm]
24 mos	20" [51 cm]

Finished chest	
6 mos	19" [48 cm]
12 mos	20" [51 cm]
18 mos	21" [53.5 cm]
24 mos	22" [56 cm]

Hat: To fit **6/12** (**18/24**) mos.

GAUGE
16 sc and 19 rows = 4" [10 cm].

ABBREVIATIONS
See page 58 for Helpful Hints.
Beg = Beginning
Ch(s) = Chain(s)
Dc = Double crochet
Dc2tog = (Yoh and draw a loop in next stitch. Yoh and draw through 2 loops on hook) twice. Yoh and draw through all loops on hook
Dc3tog = (Yoh and draw up a loop in next stitch. Yoh and draw through 2 loops on hook) 3 times. Yoh and draw through all loops on hook
Hdc = Half double crochet
Rep = Repeat
Rem = Remaining
Rnd(s) = Round(s)
RS = Right side
Sc = Single crochet
Sc2tog = Draw up a loop in each of next 2 sts. Yoh and draw through all loops on hook
Sl st = Slip stitch
Sp(s) = Space(s)
St(s) = Stitch(es)
Tog = Together
WS = Wrong side
Yoh = Yarn over hook

MATERIALS

Bernat® Softee® Baby™ (140 g /5 oz; 331 m/362 yds)

Cardigan: Boy's Version	Sizes	6	12	18	24	mos
Main Color (MC) 30044 (Flannel)		1	1	2	2	ball(s)
Contrast A 30221 (Soft Fern)		1	1	1	1	ball
Contrast B 30233 (Fresh Green)		1	1	1	1	ball
Contrast C 02000 (White)		1	1	1	1	ball
Cardigan: Girl's Version	**Sizes**	**6**	**12**	**18**	**24**	**mos**
Main Color (MC) 30044 (Flannel)		1	1	2	2	ball(s)
Contrast A 30410 (Soft Peach)		1	1	1	1	ball
Contrast B 30424 (Soft Red)		1	1	1	1	ball
Contrast C 02000 (White)		1	1	1	1	ball
Hat: Boy's Version	**Sizes**	6/12		18/24		**mos**
Main Color (MC) 30044 (Flannel) **Contrast A** 30221 (Soft Fern) **Contrast B** 30233 (Fresh Green) **Contrast C** 02000 (White)		1		1		ball
Hat: Girl's Version	**Sizes**	6/12		18/24		**mos**
Main Color (MC) 30044 (Flannel) **Contrast A** 30410 (Soft Peach) **Contrast B** 30424 (Soft Red) **Contrast C** 02000 (White)		1		1		ball

Size 4 mm (U.S. G or 6) crochet hook **or size needed to obtain gauge.** 3 buttons.

Playtime Set

INSTRUCTIONS
CARDIGAN

The instructions are written for smallest size. If changes are necessary for larger sizes the instructions will be written thus ( ). Numbers for each size are shown in the same color throughout the pattern. When only one number is given in black, it applies to all sizes.

Notes: • Cardigan is worked in one piece from the neck downwards. Sleeves are worked after. • When joining colors, work to last 2 loops on hook of first color. Draw new color through last 2 loops then proceed.
• Break yarn at end of every row, where new color was joined.

BODY

Yoke: With MC, ch 47 (51-55-59).
(See Chart V on page 42).

1st row: (RS). 1 hdc in 3rd ch from hook (counts as 1 hdc). (2 hdc in next ch. 1 hdc in next ch) 22 (24-26-28) times. Turn. Join A. 67 (73-79-85) hdc.

2nd row: With A, ch 1. 1 sc in first hdc. (Ch 2. Miss next 2 hdc. 1 sc in next hdc) 22 (24-26-28) times. Join B. Turn.

3rd row: With B, ch 3 (counts as dc). (3 dc in next ch-2 sp. Miss next sc) 21 (23-25-27) times. 3 dc in next ch-2 sp. 1 dc in last sc. Join A. Turn. 68 (74-80-86) dc.

4th row: With A, ch 1. 1 sc in first dc. 1 sc in sp between last dc and next dc. (1 sc in each of next 3 dc. 1 sc in sp between last dc and next dc) 22 (24-26-28) times. 1 sc in last dc. Join MC. Turn. 91 (99-107-115) sc.

5th row: With MC, ch 2. 1 hdc in first sc (counts as 2 hdc). Miss next sc. (2 hdc in next sc. Miss next sc) 44 (48-52-56) times. 1 hdc in last sc. Join C. Turn. 91 (99-107-115) hdc.

6th row: With C, ch 1. 1 sc in each hdc across. Join MC. Turn.

7th row: With MC, ch 2. 1 hdc in first sc (counts as 2 hdc). Miss next sc. (2 hdc in next sc. Miss next sc) 44 (48-52-56) times. 1 hdc in last sc. Join A. Turn. 91 (99-107-115) hdc.

8th row: With A, ch 1. 1 sc in each hdc across. Join B. Turn.

9th row: With B, ch 1. 1 sc in each sc across. Join C. Turn.

10th row: With C, as 9th row. Join MC. Turn.

11th row: With MC, as 9th row. Join A. Turn.

12th row: With A, ch 1. 1 sc in each of next 1 (2-1-1) sc. (Ch 2. Miss next 2 sc. 1 sc in next sc) 30 (32-35-38) times. 1 sc in each of next 0 (1-1-0) sc. Join B. Turn.

13th row: With B, ch 3 (counts as dc). 1 dc in each of next 0 (1-0-0) sc. (3 dc in next ch-2 sp. Miss next sc) 29 (31-34-37) times. 3 dc in next ch-2 sp. 1 dc in each of next 1 (2-2-1) sc. Join A. Turn. 92 (100-108-116) dc.

14th row: With A, ch 1. 1 sc in each of next 1 (2-1-1) dc. 1 sc in sp between last dc and next dc. (1 sc in each of next 3 dc. 1 sc in sp between last dc and next dc) 30 (32-35-38) times. 1 sc in each of next 1 (2-2-1) dc. Join C. Turn. 123 (133-144-155) sc.

15th row: With C, ch 1. 1 sc in each sc across. Join MC. Turn.

Divide for Body and Sleeves: 16th row: (WS). With MC, ch 1. 1 sc in each of next **14** (**14**-**15**-**15**) sc. Ch **7** (**8**-**9**-**10**). Place marker on last ch. Miss next **32** (**36**-**40**-**45**) sc. 1 sc in each of next **31** (**33**-**34**-**35**) sc. Ch **7** (**8**-**9**-**10**). Place marker on first ch. Miss next **32** (**36**-**40**-**45**) sc. 1 sc in each of next **14** (**14**-**15**-**15**) sc. Turn. **73** (**77**-**82**-**85**) sts (sc and ch) for Body.

Body: 17th row: Ch 2 (does not count as hdc). 1 hdc in first sc. (Miss next sc or ch. 2 hdc in next sc or ch) **35** (**37**-**40**-**41**) times. 1 hdc in each of next **2** (**2**-**1**-**2**) sc. Turn. **73** (**77**-**82**-**85**) hdc.
18th row: Ch 1. 1 sc in each hdc across. Turn.
19th row: Ch 2 (does not count as hdc). 1 hdc in first sc. (Miss next sc. 2 hdc in next sc) **35** (**37**-**40**-**41**) times. 1 hdc in each of next **2** (**2**-**1**-**2**) sc. Turn.
Rep 18th and 19th rows **8** (**10**-**12**-**14**) times more, then rep 18th row once.
Do **not** fasten off.

Edging: 1st rnd: With RS facing and MC, ch 1. 3 sc in first sc. 1 sc in each of next **71** (**75**-**80**-**83**) sc. 3 sc in next sc. Work **42** (**48**-**54**-**60**) sc evenly up Right Front. 3 sc in next st. *Working in rem loop of foundation ch of neck edge,* 1 sc in each of next **45** (**49**-**53**-**57**) sts. 3 sc in next st. Work **42** (**48**-**54**-**60**) sc evenly down Left Front. Join C with sl st to first sc. Break MC. **212** (**232**-**253**-**272**) sc.
2nd rnd: With C, ch 1. 1 sc in same sp as last sl st. 3 sc in next sc. 1 sc in each of next **73** (**77**-**82**-**85**) sc. 3 sc in next sc. 1 sc in each of next **44** (**50**-**56**-**62**) sc. 3 sc in next sc. 1 sc in each of next **47** (**51**-**55**-**59**) sc. 3 sc in next sc. 1 sc in each of next **43** (**49**-**55**-**61**) sc. Join A with sl st to first sc. Break C.

Boy Version: Buttonholes: 3rd rnd: With A, ch 1. 1 sc in same sp as last sl st. 3 sc in next sc. 1 sc in each of next **75** (**79**-**84**-**87**) sc. 3 sc in next sc. 1 sc in each of next **46** (**52**-**58**-**64**) sc. 3 sc in next sc. 1 sc in each of next **49** (**53**-**57**-**61**) sc. 3 sc in next sc. 1 sc in each of next 2 sc. Ch 2. Miss next 2 sc. [1 sc in each of next **4** (**6**-**7**-**9**) sc. Ch 2. Miss next 2 sc] twice. 1 sc in each sc to end of rnd. Join B with sl st to first sc. Break A.

Girl Version: Buttonholes: 3rd rnd: With A, ch 1. 1 sc in same sp as last sl st. 3 sc in next sc. 1 sc in each of next **75** (**79**-**84**-**87**) sc. 3 sc in next sc. 1 sc in each of next **30** (**32**-**36**-**38**) sc. [Ch 2. Miss next 2 sc. 1 sc in each of next **6** (**8**-**10**-**12**) sc] twice. Ch 2. Miss next 2 sc. 1 sc in each of next 2 sc. 3 sc in next sc. 1 sc in each of next **49** (**53**-**57**-**61**) sc. 3 sc in next sc. 1 sc in each of next **45** (**51**-**57**-**63**) sc. Join B with sl st to first sc. Break A.

Both Versions: 4th rnd: With B, ch 1. 1 sc in each sc or ch around. Join with sl st to first sc.
5th rnd: Ch 1. *Working from **left** to right, instead of from **right** to left as usual,* work 1 reverse sc in each sc around. Join with sl st to first st. Fasten off.

Reverse Sc

SLEEVES

Right Sleeve: With RS facing, join MC with sl st to marked ch at right armhole.

Sizes 6, 18 and 24 mos only: 1st rnd: Ch 1. 1 sc in each of next **4** (**4**-**5**) ch. Sc2tog. 1 sc in each of last **1** (**3**-**3**) ch. 1 sc in each of next **32** (**40**-**45**) sc.

Size 12 mos only: 1st rnd: Ch 1. 1 sc in each of next 4 ch. Sc2tog. 1 sc in each of last 2 ch. 1 sc in each of next 18 sc. Sc2tog. 1 sc in each of next 16 sc. Join with sl st to first sc. 42 sts.

All sizes: 2nd rnd: Ch 2 (counts as hdc). 1 hdc in same sp as last sl st. Miss next sc. (2 hdc in next sc. Miss next sc) **18 (**20**-**23**-**26**) times. Join with sl st to top of ch 2. **38** (**42**-**48**-**54**) hdc.

3rd rnd: Ch 1. [1 sc in each of next **17** (**19**-**10**-**25**) hdc. Sc2tog] **2** (**2**-**4**-**2**) times. Join with sl st to first sc. **36** (**40**-**44**-**52**) sc.

4th rnd: Ch 2 (counts as hdc). 1 hdc in same sp as last sl st. Miss next sc. (2 hdc in next sc. Miss next sc) **17** (**19**-**21**-**25**) times. Join with sl st to top of ch 2.

5th rnd: Ch 1. [1 sc in each of next **16** (**18**-**20**-**11**) hdc. Sc2tog] **2** (**2**-**2**-**4**) times. Join with sl st to first sc. **34** (**38**-**42**-**48**) sc.

6th rnd: Ch 2 (counts as hdc). 1 hdc in same sp as last sl st. Miss next sc. (2 hdc in next sc. Miss next sc) **16** (**18**-**20**-**23**) times. Join with sl st to top of ch 2.

7th rnd: Ch 1. [1 sc in each of next **15** (**17**-**19**-**22**) hdc. Sc2tog] twice. Join with sl st to first sc. **32** (**36**-**40**-**46**) sc.

8th rnd: Ch 2 (counts as hdc). 1 hdc in same sp as last sl st. Miss next sc. (2 hdc in next sc. Miss next sc) **15** (**17**-**19**-**22**) times. Join with sl st to top of ch 2.

9th rnd: Ch 1. [1 sc in each of next **14** (**16**-**18**-**21**) hdc. Sc2tog] twice. Join with sl st to first sc. **30** (**34**-**38**-**44**) sc.

10th rnd: Ch 2 (counts as hdc). 1 hdc in same sp as last sl st. Miss next sc. (2 hdc in next sc. Miss next sc) **14** (**16**-**18**-**21**) times. Join with sl st to top of ch 2.

11th rnd: Ch 1. [1 sc in each of next **13** (**15**-**17**-**20**) hdc. Sc2tog] twice. Join with sl st to first sc. **28** (**32**-**36**-**42**) sc.

12th rnd: Ch 2 (counts as hdc). 1 hdc in same sp as last sl st. Miss next sc. (2 hdc in next sc. Miss next sc) **13** (**15**-**17**-**20**) times. Join with sl st to top of ch 2.

13th rnd: Ch 1. [1 sc in each of next **12** (**14**-**16**-**19**) hdc. Sc2tog] twice. Join with sl st to first sc. **26** (**30**-**34**-**40**) sc.

14th rnd: Ch 2 (counts as hdc). 1 hdc in same sp as last sl st. Miss next sc. (2 hdc in next sc. Miss next sc) **12** (**14**-**16**-**19**) times. Join with sl st to top of ch 2.

15th rnd: Ch 1. [1 sc in each of next **11** (**13**-**15**-**18**) hdc. Sc2tog] twice. Join with sl st to first sc. **24** (**28**-**32**-**38**) sc.

16th rnd: Ch 2 (counts as hdc). 1 hdc in same sp as last sl st. Miss next sc. (2 hdc in next sc. Miss next sc) **11** (**13**-**15**-**18**) times. Join with sl st to top of ch 2.

Sizes 12, 18 and 24 mos only: 17th rnd: Ch 1. [1 sc in each of next (**12**-**14**-**17**) hdc. Sc2tog] twice. Join with sl st to first sc. (**26**-**30**-**36**) sc.

18th rnd: Ch 2 (counts as hdc). 1 hdc in same sp as last sl st. Miss next sc. (2 hdc in next sc. Miss next sc) (**12**-**14**-**17**) times. Join with sl st to top of ch 2.

19th rnd: Ch 1. [1 sc in each of next (**11**-**13**-**16**) hdc. Sc2tog] twice. Join with sl st to first sc. (**24**-**28**-**34**) sc.

20th rnd: Ch 2 (counts as hdc). 1 hdc in same sp as last sl st. Miss next sc. (2 hdc in next sc. Miss next sc) (**11**-**13**-**16**) times. Join with sl st to top of ch 2.

Sizes 18 and 24 mos only: 21st rnd: Ch 1. [1 sc in each of next (**12**-**15**) hdc. Sc2tog] twice. Join with sl st to first sc. (**26**-**32**) sc.

22nd rnd: Ch 2 (counts as hdc). 1 hdc in same sp as last sl st. Miss next sc. (2 hdc in next sc. Miss next sc) (**12**-**15**) times. Join with sl st to top of ch 2.

Size 24 mos only: 23rd rnd: Ch 1. (1 sc in each of next 14 hdc. Sc2tog) twice. Join with sl st to first sc. 30 sc.

24th rnd: Ch 2 (counts as hdc). 1 hdc in same sp as last sl st. Miss next sc. (2 hdc in next sc. Miss next sc) 14 times. Join with sl st to top of ch 2.

All Sizes: Next rnd: Join C, ch 1. 1 sc in each st around. Join A with sl st to first sc. **22** (**24**-**26**-**30**) sc.

Next rnd: With A, ch 1. 1 sc in each sc around. Join B with sl st to first sc.

Next rnd: With B, ch 1. 1 sc in each sc around. Join with sl st to first sc.

Next rnd: Ch 1. *Working from **left** to right, instead of from **right** to left as usual,* work 1 reverse sc in each sc around. Join with sl st to first st. Fasten off.**

Left Sleeve: With RS facing, join MC with sl st to marked st.

Sizes 6, 18 and 24 mos only: 1st rnd: Ch 1. 1 sc in each of next 32 (40-45) sc. 1 sc in each of next 1 (3-3) ch. Sc2tog. 1 sc in each of last 4 (4-5) ch. 38 (48-54) sc.

Size 12 mos only: 1st rnd: Ch 1. 1 sc in each of next 16 sc. Sc2tog. 1 sc in each of next 18 sc. 1 sc in each of next 2 ch. Sc2tog. 1 sc in each of last 4 ch. Join with sl st to first sc. 42 sc.

All sizes: Work from ** to ** as given for Right Sleeve.

FINISHING

Decorative Top Stitch (yoke): ***With RS of Cardigan facing, join C with sl st around post of first sc of any row worked with C. Sl st around post of each sc across. Fasten off.***
Rep for rem 2 rows worked with C.

Sew buttons to correspond to buttonholes.

HAT

Band: With MC, ch 6.
1st row: 1 sc in 2nd ch from hook. 1 sc in each ch to end of chain. Turn. 5 sc.
2nd row: Ch 1. *Working in back loops only,* 1 sc in each sc across. Turn.
Rep 2nd row until work from beg measures 17½ (19½)" [44.5 (49.5) cm]. Fasten off.
Sew foundation ch and last row tog.

Beg working in rnds: Join MC with sl st at seam.
1st rnd: (RS). Ch 1. Work 70 (80) sc evenly around edge of band. Join with sl st to first sc.
2nd rnd: Ch 2 (counts as hdc). 1 hdc in same sp as last sl st. Miss next sc. (2 hdc in next sc. Miss next sc) 34 (39) times. Join with sl st to top of ch 2. 70 (80) hdc.
3rd rnd: Ch 1. 1 sc in each hdc around. Join with sl st to first sc.
4th rnd: Ch 2 (counts as hdc). 1 hdc in same sp as last sl st. Miss next sc. (2 hdc in next sc. Miss next sc) 34 (39) times. Join with sl st to top of ch 2.
Rep 3rd and 4th rnds 1 (2) time(s) more, joining C at end of last rnd. Break MC.

Next rnd: With C, ch 1. 1 sc in each hdc around. Join B with sl st to first sc.
Next rnd: With B, ch 1. [1 sc in each of next 5 (6) sc. Sc2tog] 10 times. Join A with sl st to first sc. 60 (70) sc.
Next rnd: With A, ch 1. 1 sc in each st around. Join MC with sl st to first sc.

Next rnd: With MC, ch 2 (counts as hdc). 1 hdc in same sp as last sl st. Miss next sc. (2 hdc in next sc. Miss next sc) **29** (**34**) times. Join C with sl st to first sc.

Next rnd: With C, ch 1. 1 sc in each hdc around. Join MC with sl st to first sc.

Next rnd: With MC, ch 2 (counts as hdc). 1 hdc in same sp as last sl st. Miss next sc. (2 hdc in next sc. Miss next sc) **29** (**34**) times. Join A with sl st to first sc.

Next rnd: With A, ch 1. 1 sc in first sc. Ch 2. Miss 2 hdc. (1 sc in next sc. Ch 2. Miss next 2 hdc) **19** (**22**) times. (1 sc in next sc. Ch 2. Miss next 3 hdc) **0** (**1**) time. Join with sl st to first sc. Fasten off.

Next rnd: Join B with sl st to any ch-2 sp. (Ch 2. Dc2tog) in same sp as last sl st. (Miss next sc. Dc3tog) **19** (**23**) times. Join A with sl st to first sc.

Next rnd: With A, ch 1. 1 sc in first st. 1 sc in sp between last st and next st. (1 sc in next st. 1 sc in sp between last st and next st) **19** (**23**) times. Join MC with sl st to first sc. **40** (**48**) sc.

Next rnd: With MC, ch 1. (1 sc in each of next 2 sc. Sc2tog) **10** (**12**) times. Join with sl st to first sc. **30** (**36**) sc.

Next rnd: Ch 2 (counts as hdc). 1 hdc in same sp as last sl st. Miss next sc. (2 hdc in next sc. Miss next sc) **14** (**17**) times. Join with sl st to top of ch 2. **30** (**36**) hdc.

Next rnd: Ch 1. (Sc2tog) **15** (**18**) times. Join with sl st to first sc. **15** (**18**) sts.

Next rnd: Ch 1. (Sc2tog) **7** (**9**) times. 1 sc in each of next **1** (**0**) sc. Join with sl st to first sc. Fasten off. Thread yarn through rem sts. Pull tightly and fasten securely.

FINISHING

Decorative Top Stitch: Work from *** to *** as given for Cardigan.

Rep for rem row with C. BERNAT

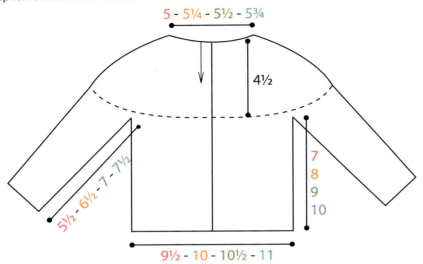

Chart V

NOTE: RED STITCHES ONLY OCCUR IN SOME SIZES

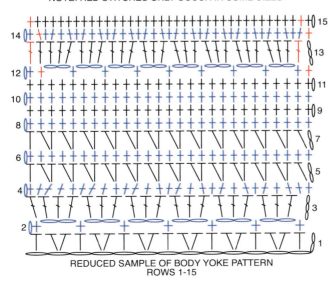

REDUCED SAMPLE OF BODY YOKE PATTERN
ROWS 1-15

Key

◯ = chain (ch)

✛ = single crochet (sc)

T = half double crochet (hdc)

Ŧ = double crochet (dc)

6. Super Stripes Set

SIZES
Pullover

To fit chest measurement	
6 mos	17" [43 cm]
12 mos	18" [45.5 cm]
18 mos	19" [48 cm]
24 mos	20" [51 cm]

Finished chest	
6 mos	19" [48 cm]
12 mos	20" [51 cm]
18 mos	21" [53.5 cm]
24 mos	23" [58.5 cm]

Hat: To fit 6/12 (18/24) mos.

MATERIALS

Bernat® Softee® Baby™ (140 g /5 oz; 331 m/362 yds)						
Pullover	**Sizes**	6	12	18	24	mos
	Main Color (MC) (30201 Aqua)	1	1	2	2	ball(s)
	Contrast A (30044 Flannel)	1	1	1	2	ball(s)
Hat	**Sizes**	6/12		18/24		mos
	Main Color (MC) (30201 Aqua)	1		1		ball
	Contrast A (30044 Flannel)	1		1		ball
Size 4 mm (U.S. G or 6) crochet hook **or size needed to obtain gauge.**						

ABBREVIATIONS

See page 58 for Helpful Hints.
Alt = Alternate(ing)
Approx = Approximately
Beg = Beginning
Ch(s) = Chain(s)
Cont = Continue(ity)
Dc = Double crochet
Hdc = Half double crochet
Pat = Pattern
Rem = Remaining
Rep = Repeat
RS = Right side
Sc = Single crochet
Sc2tog = Draw up a loop in each of next 2 sts. Yoh and draw through all loops on hook
Sl st = Slip stitch
Sp(s) = Space(s)
St(s) = Stitch(es)
WS = Wrong side
Yoh = Yarn over hook

GAUGE

16 sc and 19 rows = 4" [10 cm].

INSTRUCTIONS

PULLOVER

Notes: Ch 2 at beg of row does not count as hdc.
• To join new color, work to last 2 loops on hook. Draw new color through last 2 loops then proceed in new color.

The instructions are written for smallest size. If changes are necessary for larger sizes the instructions will be written thus ( ). Numbers for each size are shown in the same color throughout the pattern. When only one number is given in black, it applies to all sizes.

BACK

Ribbing: With MC, ch **7 (**8**-**9**-**9**).
1st row: (RS). 1 sc in 2nd ch from hook. 1 sc in each ch to end of chain. Turn. **6** (**7**-**8**-**8**) sc.
2nd row: Ch 1. *Working in back loops only,* 1 sc in each sc to end of row. Turn.
Rep last row until work from beg measures **9½** (**10**-**10½**-**11½**)" [**24** (**25.5**-**26.5**-**29**) cm], when slightly stretched. Fasten off.

1st row: (RS). Join A with sl st to top right corner. *Working across long side of ribbing,* ch 2. 1 hdc in same sp as sl st. Work **37** (**39**-**41**-**45**) hdc across. **38** (**40**-**42**-**46**) hdc. Turn.
2nd row: Ch 2. 1 hdc in each hdc to end of row. Join MC. Turn.
3rd row: With MC, ch 1. 1 sc in each hdc to end of row. Turn.
4th row: Ch 1. 1 sc in each sc to end of row. Join A. Turn.
5th row: With A, ch 2. 1 hdc in each hdc to end of row. Turn.
Rep 2nd to 5th rows for Stripe Pat until work from beg measures approx **6½** (**7½**-**8**-**9**)" [**16.5** (**19**-**20.5**-**23**) cm], ending with 4th row of pat. Fasten off.

Shape armholes: 1st row: (RS). Miss first **4** (**4**-**5**-**5**) sc. Join A to next sc. Keeping cont of Stripe Pat, ch 2. 1 hdc in same sp as sl st. 1 hdc in each sc to last **4** (**4**-**5**-**5**) sc. **Turn.** Leave rem sts unworked.**
Cont even in pat on rem **30** (**32**-**32**-**36**) sts until armhole measures approx **4½** (**5**-**5½**-**6**)" [**11.5** (**12.5**-**14**-**15**) cm], ending with a WS row. Fasten off.

FRONT

Work from ** to ** as given for Back.

Proceed as follows:

Shape Placket opening: 1st row: (WS). With A, ch 2. 1 hdc in each of next **9** (**9-9-11**) hdc. Join MC. **Turn.** Leave rem sts unworked.

Work on rem **9** (**9-9-11**) sts for **left side** as follows:

2nd row: With MC, ch 1. Sc2tog. 1 sc in each hdc to end of row. Turn.

3rd row: Ch 1. 1 sc in each st to end of row. Join A. Turn.

4th and 5th rows: With A, ch 2. 1 hdc in each st to end of row. Join MC at end of 5th row. Turn.

Rep last 4 rows **1** (**1-1-2**) time(s) more. **7** (**7-7-8**) sts rem.

Cont even in pat until armhole measures same length as Back before shoulder, ending with same row of pat as Back. Fasten off.

With WS facing, miss next **12** (**14-14-14**) hdc. Join A with sl st to next hdc. Ch 2. 1 hdc in same sp as sl st. 1 hdc in each hdc to end of row. Join MC. Turn.

Work on rem **9** (**9-9-11**) sts for **right side** as follows:

2nd row: With MC, ch 1. 1 sc in each hdc to last 2 hdc. Sc2tog. Turn.

3rd row: Ch 1. 1 sc in each st to end of row. Join A. Turn.

4th and 5th rows: With A, ch 2. 1 hdc in each st to end of row. Join MC at end of 5th row. Turn.

Rep last 4 rows **1** (**1-1-2**) time(s) more. **7** (**7-7-8**) sts rem.

Cont even in pat until armhole measures same length as Back before shoulder, ending with same row of pat as Back. Fasten off.

SLEEVES

Ribbing: With MC, ch **6** (**7**-**7**-**7**).
1st row: (RS). 1 sc in 2nd ch from hook. 1 sc in each ch to end of chain. Turn. **5** (**6**-**6**-**6**) sc.
2nd row: Ch 1. *Working in back loops only,* 1 sc in each sc to end of row. Turn.
Rep last row until work from beg measures **7** (**7½**-**7½**-**8**)" [**18** (**19**-**19**-**20.5**) cm], when slightly stretched. Fasten off.
1st row: (RS). Join A with sl st to top right corner. *Working across long side of ribbing,* ch 2. 1 hdc in same sp as sl st. Work **27** (**29**-**29**-**33**) hdc across. **28** (**30**-**30**-**34**) hdc.
2nd row: Ch 2. 1 hdc in each hdc to end of row. Join MC. Turn.
3rd row: With MC, ch 1. 2 sc in first hdc. 1 sc in each hdc to last hdc. 2 sc in last hdc. Turn.
4th row: Ch 1. 1 sc in each sc to end of row. Join A. Turn.
5th and 6th rows: With A, ch 2. 1 hdc in each st to end of row. Join MC at end of 6th row. Turn.
Rep last 4 rows **3** (**4**-**6**-**6**) times more. **36** (**40**-**44**-**48**) sts. Place marker at end of last row. Work **3** (**3**-**4**-**4**) more rows even in pat. Fasten off.

FINISHING

Pin garment pieces to measurements and cover with damp cloth leaving cloth to dry.

Collar: Sew shoulder seams.
1st row: With RS facing, join MC with sl st to front loop of first st of placket opening. Ch 1. 1 sc in same sp as sl st. *Working in front loops only,* 1 sc in each of next **11** (**13**-**13**-**13**) sts. Turn.
2nd row: Ch 1. *Working in back loops only,* 1 sc in each sc across. Turn.
Rep last row until work measures length to fit around neck edge (without stretching), ending with a WS row. Fasten off.
Sew last row behind front to rem back loops of first row. Sew Collar along neck edge.

Sew in sleeves, placing rows above markers along armhole edges of Fronts and Back to form square armholes. Sew side and sleeve seams.

HAT

Ribbing: With MC, ch 13.
1st row: (RS). 1 sc in 2nd ch from hook. 1 sc in each ch to end of chain. Turn. 12 sc.
2nd row: Ch 1. *Working in back loops only,* 1 sc in each sc to end of row. Turn.
Rep last row until work from beg measures **16** (**17½**)" [**40.5** (**44.5**) cm], when slightly stretched. Fasten off.
1st rnd: (RS). Join A with sl st to top right corner. *Working across long side of ribbing,* ch 3 (counts as dc). Work **63** (**67**) dc across. Place marker at end of last row. **64** (**68**) dc. Join MC with sl st to first dc.
2nd rnd: With MC, ch 1. 1 sc in each dc around. Join A with sl st to first sc.
3rd rnd: With A, ch 3. 1 dc in each dc around. Join MC with sl st to first dc.
Last 2 rnds form Stripe Pat.

Cont in Stripe Pat until work from marked rnd measures approx **3½** (**3¾**)" [**9** (**9.5**) cm], ending with 3rd rnd of pat.

Shape top: 1st rnd: With MC, ch 1. *1 sc in each of next **14** (**15**) dc. Sc2tog. Rep from * around. Join A with sl st to first sc.
2nd and alt rnds: With A, ch 3. 1 dc in each st around. Join MC with sl st to first dc.
3rd rnd: With MC, ch 1. *1 sc in each of next **13** (**14**) dc. Sc2tog. Rep from * around. Join A with sl st to first sc.
5th rnd: With MC, ch 1. *1 sc in each of next **12** (**13**) dc. Sc2tog. Rep from * around. Join A with sl st to first sc.
Cont in same manner until 20 sts rem. Work 6 rnds even in pat. Fasten off. Sew top seam flat.

Pom-pom: Wind yarn around 3 fingers approx 60 times. Remove from fingers and tie tightly in center. Cut through each side of loops. Trim to a smooth round shape. Sew pom-pom to top of Hat. BERNAT

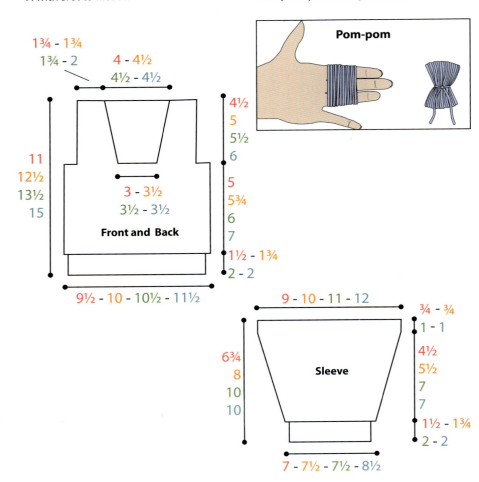

7. Top Down Cuties

SIZES
Cardigan

To fit chest measurement	
6 mos	16-17" [40.5 – 43 cm]
12 mos	17-18" [43 – 45.5 cm]
18 mos	18-19" [45.5 – 48 cm]
24 mos	19-20" [48 – 51 cm]

Finished chest	
6 mos	20½" [52 cm]
12 mos	22" [56 cm]
18 mos	22½" [57 cm]
24 mos	23½" [59.5 cm]

Hat
To fit 6/12 (18/24) mos

ABBREVIATIONS
See page 58 for Helpful Hints.
Alt = Alternate(ing)
Approx = Approximately
Beg = Beginning
Cont = Continue(ity)
Dec = Decrease(ing)
K = Knit
K2tog = Knit next 2 stitches together
Pat = Pattern
P = Purl
Rep = Repeat
RS = Right side
St(s) = Stitch(es)
WS = Wrong side
Yo = Yarn over

MATERIALS

Bernat® Softee® Baby™ (Ombres: 120 g/4.25 oz; 283 m/310 yds)					
Cardigan Sizes	6	12	18	24	mos
31201 (Prince Pebbles) OR 31425 (Princess Pebbles)	2	2	3	3	balls
Hat Sizes	6/12		18/24		mos
31201 (Prince Pebbles) OR 31425 (Princess Pebbles)	1		1		ball

Size 4 mm (U.S. 6) knitting needles. Size 4 mm (U.S. 6) circular knitting needle 24" [60 cm] long **or size needed to obtain gauge.** 2 stitch holders. 4 buttons.

GAUGE

21 sts and 40 rows = 4" [10 cm] in garter stitch.

INSTRUCTIONS

The instructions are written for smallest size. If changes are necessary for larger sizes the instructions will be written thus ( ). Numbers for each size are shown in the same color throughout the pattern. When only one number is given in black, it applies to all sizes.

CARDIGAN

Note: Body is worked in one piece from the neck edge down.

BODY

With pair of needles, cast on **52** (**56**-**56**-**64**) sts.

1st row: (RS). K**11** (**12**-**12**-**13**). Place marker. K**8** (**8**-**8**-**10**). Place marker. K**14** (**16**-**16**-**18**). Place marker. K**8** (**8**-**8**-**10**). Place marker. K**11** (**12**-**12**-**13**).

2nd row: Knit.

3rd row: *K2. yo. K2tog* – buttonhole made. *Knit to 1 st before marker. yo. K1. Slip marker. K1. yo. Rep from * 3 times more. Knit to end of row.

4th row: Knit.

5th row: *Knit to 1 st before marker. yo. K1. Slip marker. K1. yo. Rep from * 3 times more. Knit to end of row.

Rep last 2 rows **16** (**16**-**17**-**15**) times more, AT THE SAME TIME working buttonholes at beg of every following **12th** (**14th**-**14th**-**16th**) row from first buttonhole row 3 times more, changing to circular needle when necessary to accomodate extra sts. **196** (**200**-**208**-**200**) sts.

Next 3 rows: Knit.

Next row: (RS). *Knit to 1 st before marker. yo. K1. Slip marker. K1. yo. Rep from * 3 times more. Knit to end of row.

Rep last 4 rows **0** (**1**-**1**-**3**) times more. **204** (**216**-**224**-**232**) sts.

Divide for Sleeves:

Next row: (WS). K**30** (**32**-**33**-**34**) for Left Front. K**46** (**48**-**50**-**52**) and slip these **46** (**48**-**50**-**52**) sts to st holder for Left Sleeve. Cast on 2 sts. K**52** (**56**-**58**-**60**) sts for Back. K**46** (**48**-**50**-**52**) and slip these **46** (**48**-**50**-**52**) sts to st holder for Right Sleeve. Cast on 2 sts. K**30** (**32**-**33**-**34**) for Right Front. **116** (**124**-**128**-**132**) sts.

Cont even in garter st (knit every row) until work from divide measures **6½** (**7**-**7½** -**8**)" [**16.5** (**18**-**19**-**20.5**) cm], ending with a RS row. Cast off.

RIGHT SLEEVE

1st row: (RS). With circular needle, cast on 1 st. K**46** (**48**-**50**-**52**) from Right Sleeve st holder. **Do not join.**

2nd row: Cast on 1 st. Knit to end of row. K48** (**50**-**52**-**54**) sts.

Cont in garter st, dec 1 st each end of next and every following **10th** (**10th**-**10th**-**12th**) row to **36** (**38**-**40**-**42**) sts.

Cont even in garter st until Sleeve measures **6½** (**7**-**7½**-**8**)" [**16.5** (**18**-**19**-**20.5**) cm] ending with a RS row. Cast off.**

LEFT SLEEVE

1st row: (RS). With circular needle, cast on 1 st. K**46** (**48**-**50**-**52**) from Left Sleeve st holder. **Do not join.**

Work from ** to ** as given for Right Sleeve.

FINISHING

Sew Sleeve and underarm seams.
Sew buttons to Left Front to correspond with buttonholes.

HAT

With pair of larger needles, cast on **73** (**81**) sts.

Work in garter st (knit every row) noting 1st row is RS until work from beg measures **4½** (**5**)" [**11.5** (**12.5**) cm], ending with a WS row.

Shape top: 1st row: (RS). K1. *K2tog. K**7** (**8**). Rep from * to end of row. **65** (**73**) sts.

2nd and alt rows: Knit.

3rd row: K1. *K2tog. K**6** (**7**). Rep from * to end of row. **55** (**65**) sts.

5th row: K1. *K2tog. K**5** (**6**). Rep from * to end of row. **49** (**57**) sts.

7th row: K1. *K2tog. K**4** (**5**). Rep from * to end of row. **41** (**49**) sts.

9th row: K1. *K2tog. K**3** (**4**). Rep from * to end of row. **33** (**41**) sts.

11th row: K1. *K2tog. K**2** (**3**). Rep from * to end of row. **25** (**33**) sts.

13th row: K1. *K2tog. K**1** (**2**). Rep from * to end of row. **17** (**25**) sts.

15th row: K1. *K2tog. K**0** (**1**). Rep from * to end of row. **9** (**17**) sts.

Size 18/24 mos only: 16th row: Knit.
17th row: K1. *K2tog. Rep from * to end of row. **9** sts.

Both sizes: Break yarn leaving a long end. Thread end through rem sts and gather tightly. Fasten securely. Sew seam.

Pom-pom: Wind yarn around 3 fingers approx 80 times. Remove from fingers and tie tightly in center. Cut through each side of loops. Trim to a smooth round shape. Sew pom-pom to top of Hat. **BERNAT**

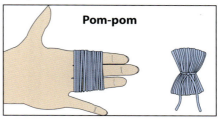
Pom-pom

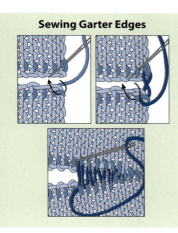
Sewing Garter Edges

Thread yarn end through blunt ended large eye needle. Working with the right side facing, insert needle into first ridge at bottom of work. Draw needle through ridge on opposite side of seam. Continue drawing needle through alternating ridges at each side of seam.
After you have joined a few rows, pull the yarn, but not too tightly, to merge the 2 sides together (tog).
Continue the process to the end of seam. Cut the yarn leaving a 6" [15 cm] end. Weave the end into seam.

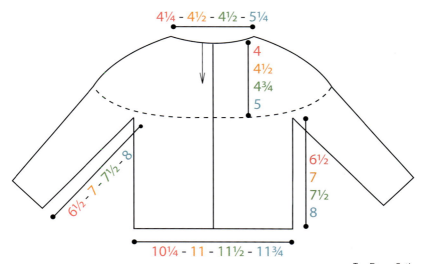

Top Down Cuties

8. Just Peachy Blankie

CIRCULAR NEEDLE | LIGHT | INTERMEDIATE

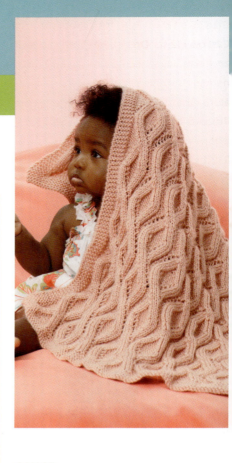

MEASUREMENT
Approx 30" [76 cm] square.

ABBREVIATIONS
See page 58 for Helpful Hints.
Alt = Alternate(ing)
Approx = Approximately
Beg = Beginning
Dec = Decrease(ing)
Inc = Increase(ing)
K = Knit
K2tog = Knit next 2 stitches together
K3togtbl = Knit next 3 stitches together through back loops
P = Purl
Pat = Pattern
Rep = Repeat
Ssk = Slip next 2 stitches knitwise one at a time. Pass them back onto left-hand needle, then knit through back loops together
WS = Wrong side
Yo = Yarn over

GAUGE
22 sts and 30 rows = 4" [10 cm] in stocking st.

MATERIALS

Bernat® Softee® Baby™ (140 g /5 oz; 331 m/362 yds)	
30410 (Soft Peach)	**2 balls**
Size 4 mm (U.S. 6) circular knitting needle 36" [90 cm] long **or size needed to obtain gauge.**	

INSTRUCTIONS

Cast on 132 sts. **Do not** join. Working back and forth across needle in rows, knit 7 rows, noting 1st row is WS and inc 10 sts evenly across last row. 142 sts.

Proceed in pat as follows:

(See Chart VI on page 57).

1st row: (RS). K5. P2. *P3. K1. yo. K2. ssk. P3. yo. K2. ssk. P7. K2tog. K2. yo. Rep from * to last 5 sts. K5.

2nd and alt rows: K5. Knit all knit sts and yo sts and purl all purl sts as they appear to last 5 sts. K5.

3rd row: K5. P2. *P2. K3. yo. K2. ssk. P3. yo. K2. ssk. P5. K2tog. K2. yo. P1. Rep from * to last 5 sts. K5.

5th row: K5. P2. *P1. K2tog. K2. yo. P1. yo. K2. ssk. P3. yo. K2. ssk. P3. K2tog. K2. yo. P2. Rep from * to last 5 sts. K5.

7th row: K5. P2. *K2tog. K2. yo. P3. yo. K2. ssk. P3. yo. K2. ssk. P1. K2tog. K2. yo. P3. Rep from * to last 5 sts. K5.

9th row: K5. *P1. K2tog. K2. yo. P5. yo. K2. ssk. P3. yo. K2. K3togtbl. K2. yo. P2. Rep from * to last 7 sts. P2. K5.

11th row: K5. *K2tog. K2. yo. P7. yo. K2. ssk. P3. yo. K2. K3togtbl. yo. P3. Rep from * to last 7 sts. P2. K5.

13th row: K5. *yo. K2. ssk. P7. K2tog. K2. yo. P3. K1. yo. K2. ssk. P3. Rep from * to last 7 sts. P2. K5.

15th row: K5. *P1. yo. K2. ssk. P5. K2tog. K2. yo. P3. K3. yo. K2. ssk. P2. Rep from * to last 7 sts. P2. K5.

17th row: K5. P2. *yo. K2. ssk. P3. K2tog. K2. yo. P3. K2tog. K2. yo. P1. yo. K2. ssk. P3. Rep from * to last 5 sts. K5.

19th row: K5. P2. *P1. yo. K2. ssk. P1. K2tog. K2. yo. P3. K2tog. K2. yo. P3. yo. K2. ssk. P2. Rep from * to last 5 sts. K5.

21st row: K5. P2. *P2. yo. K2. K3togtbl. K2. yo. P3. K2tog. K2. yo. P5. yo. K2. ssk. P1. Rep from * to last 5 sts. K5.

23rd row: K5. P2. *P3. yo. K2. K3togtbl. yo. P3. K2tog. K2. yo. P7. yo. K2. ssk. Rep from * to last 5 sts. K5.

24th row: As 2nd row.

Rep these 1st to 24th rows for pat until work from beg measures approx 29' [73.5 cm], ending with 24th row of pat.

Next row: (RS). Knit, dec 10 sts evenly across. 132 sts.

Knit 6 rows (garter st).

Cast off knitwise (WS). BERNAT

Chart VI

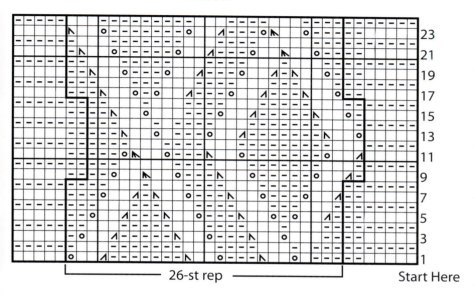

26-st rep

Start Here

Key

☐ = Knit on RS row. Purl on WS rows.

− = Purl on RS row. Knit on WS row.

○ = yo

⟈ = ssk

⟋ = K2tog

⟈ = K3togtbl

Just Peachy Blankie 57

Helpful Hints

Bernat® Softee® Baby™
Solids #166030: 100% Acrylic (140 g / 5 oz)
Ombres #166031: 100% Acrylic (120 g / 4.25 oz)

WASHING AND CARE INSTRUCTIONS
Machine Washing: Wash in water (not exceeding 40°C/104°F) at permanent press setting. Do not use bleach.
Machine Drying: Tumble dry at low heat, at delicate setting.
Do not iron or press. Do not overheat.

Pulling Yarn: To start a ball of yarn, use one of the following methods:

1. From the center
2. Start the project from the outside tail

See Video at: www.bernat.com/videos

U.S. Knitters Please Note: Canadian and American terminologies differ slightly. Equivalents are shown.

Canadian	U.S.
cast off	bind off
tension	gauge

* = The star symbol is a repeat sign and means that you follow the printed instructions from the first * until you reach the second *. You will then repeat from * to * the given number of times which does not include the first time. The ** and *** are used in the same way.

ABBREVIATIONS: cm = centimeter(s), g = gram(s), " = inch(es), m = meter(s), mm = millimeter(s), oz = ounce(s), 0 = no stitches, times or rows

GAUGE SWATCH
For best results, be sure to use the yarn recommended in the pattern, and purchase enough of one dye lot to complete your project. It is a good idea to retain ball bands in case of inquiry. Before you begin to knit or crochet, check your gauge by making a test swatch and adjusting your needle or hook size, if necessary, to obtain the gauge quoted in the pattern. Inaccurate gauge results in an item too large or too small. Even a variation of half a stitch makes an obvious difference in the finished size.

(Example knit gauge swatch shown: 17 sts and 21 rows).

Helpful Hints

DETERMINING SIZE
CHILD SIZES: Begin with chest measurement. Compare measurement to the 'To fit chest measurement' size line in your pattern and choose the closest match.

Chest Measurement (A)
Measure crease right under underarm, keeping the tape straight across the back.

Waist Measurement (B)
Tie a piece of string around the child's waist as a guide line. If you have problems finding the natural waistline, bend child sideways – the crease that forms is the waistline.

Wrist to Underarm (C)
Measure from the wrist along the inside of the arm to approximately 1 inch [2.5 cm] from the underarm crease. This is the measurement for the sleeve.

Skill Levels

BEGINNER — Projects for first-time knitters or crocheters using basic stitches. Minimal shaping.

EASY — Projects using basic stitches, repetitive stitch patterns, simple color changes, simple shaping and finishing.

INTERMEDIATE — Projects with a variety of stitches and techniques such as basic cables and lace, simple intarsia and double pointed needles for knitting. Crochet projects may involve basic lace patterns or color-patterns, mid-level shaping and finishing.

EXPERIENCED — Projects using advanced techniques and stitches such as short rows, fair isle, more intricate intarsia and cables and numerous color changes for knitting. Crochet projects may involve non repeating patterns, multi-color techniques, fine threads, small hooks, detailed shaping and refined finishing.

Crochet Hook Conversion Chart

Canadian & U.K. Sizes	000	00	0	2	3	4	5	6	7	8	-	9	10	11	-	12	13	14
Metric Sizes (mm)	10	9	8	7	6.50	6	5.50	5	4.50	4	3.75	3.5	3.25	3	2.75	2.5	2.25	2
U.S. Sizes	N 15	M 13	L 11	-	K 10½	J 10	I 9	H 8	7	G 6	F 5	E 4	D 3	-	C 2	-	B 1	-

Knitting Needle Conversion Chart

Canadian & U.K. Sizes	-	-	000	00	0	1	2	3	4	5	6	7	8	9	-	10	11	12	13	14	15
Metric Sizes (mm)	15	12.75	10	9	8	7.5	7	6.5	6	5.5	5	4.5	4	3.75	3.5	3.25	2.75	2.5	2.25	2	1.75
U.S. Sizes	19	17	15	13	11	-	-	10½	10	9	8	7	6	5	4	3	-	2	1	0	-

Learn to Knit Instructions

Casting On

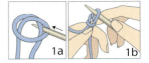 

1a Make a slip knot: Loop the yarn as shown and slip needle under the lower strand of the loop.

1b Pull up a loop of yarn.

2 Pull the yarn end attached to the ball of yarn to tighten the slip knot leaving the other end approx 4 ins [10 cm] long. Transfer needle to left hand.

3a Insert the right-hand needle through slip knot and wind yarn over right-hand needle.

3b Pull loop through slip knot.

 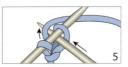 

4 Place new loop on left-hand needle. [You now have 2 stitches (sts) on your left-hand needle].

5 Insert right-hand needle between last 2 stitches (sts) on left-hand needle and wind yarn over right-hand needle.

6 Pull loop through. Place this new loop on left-hand needle beside last stitch (st). (You now have 1 more stitch on left-hand needle). Repeat (rep) steps 5 and 6 until required number of stitches (sts) have been cast on left-hand needle.

The Knit Stitch

1 Hold the needle with cast on stitches (sts) in your left hand, and the loose yarn attached to the ball at the back of work. Insert right-hand needle from left to right through the front of the first stitch (st) on the left-hand needle.

2 Wind the yarn from left to right over the point of the right-hand needle.

3 Draw the yarn through this original stitch (st) which forms a new stitch (st) on right-hand needle.

4 Slip the original stitch (st) off the left-hand needle, keeping the new stitch (st) on the right-hand needle.

5 To knit a row, repeat steps 1 to 4 until all stitches (sts) have been transferred from left-hand needle to right-hand needle. Turn the work by transferring the needle with stitches (sts) into your left hand to knit the next row.

Learn to Knit Instructions

The Purl Stitch

1 With yarn at front of work, insert right-hand needle from right to left through front of first stitch (st) on left-hand needle.

2 Wind yarn around right-hand needle. Pull yarn through stitch (st).

3 Slip original stitch (st) off needle. Repeat (rep) these steps until all stitches (sts) on left-hand needle have been transferred onto right-hand needle to complete one row of purling.

Increasing and Decreasing

Increase 1 stitch (st) in next stitch (st) Work into front and back of stitch (st) as follows: Knit stitch (st), then before slipping it off needle, twist right-hand needle behind left-hand needle and knit again into back of loop. Slip original stitch (st) off needle. There are now 2 stitches (sts) on right-hand needle made from original stitch.

K2tog Decrease Knit 2 stitches (sts) together (tog) through the front of both loops.

P2tog Decrease Purl 2 stitches (sts) together (tog) through the front of both loops.

Casting Off

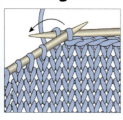

Cast off using knit stitch (knitwise) Knit the first 2 stitches (sts). *Using left-hand needle, lift first stitch (st) over second stitch (st) and drop it off between points of the 2 needles. Knit the next stitch (st); repeat (rep) from * until all stitches (sts) from left-hand needle have been worked and only 1 stitch (st) remains on the right-hand needle. Cut yarn (leaving enough to sew in end) and thread cut end through stitch (st) on needle. Draw yarn up firmly to fasten off last stitch (st).

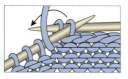

Cast off using purl stitch (purlwise) Purl first 2 stitches (sts). *Using left-hand needle, lift first stitch (st) over second stitch (st) and drop it off needle. Purl next stitch (st); repeat (rep) from * securing the last stitch (st) as described for casting off knitwise.

Learn to Crochet Instructions

Slip Knot

1 Make a loop, then hook another loop through it.

2 Tighten gently and slide the knot up to the hook.

Chain Stitch (ch)

1 Yarn over hook (yoh) and draw the yarn through to form a new loop without tightening up the previous one.

2 Repeat to form as many chains (ch) as required. Do not count the slip knot as a stitch.

Slip Stitch (sl st)

This is the shortest crochet stitch and unlike other stitches is not used on its own to produce a fabric. It is used for joining, shaping and where necessary carrying the yarn to another part of the fabric for the next stage.

Insert hook into work (second chain from hook), yarn over hook (yoh) and draw the yarn through both the work and loop on hook in one movement.

To join a chain ring with a slip stitch (sl st), insert hook into first chain (ch), yarn over hook (yoh) and draw through both the work and the yarn on hook in one movement.

Single Crochet (sc)

1 Insert the hook into the work [2nd chain (ch) from hook on starting chain], *yarn over hook (yoh) and draw yarn through the work only.

2 Yarn over hook (yoh) again and draw the yarn through both loops on the hook.

3 1 single crochet (sc) made. Insert hook into next stitch: repeat (rep) from * in step 1.